CHATHAM HOUSE PAPERS

THE
SOVIET UNION
AND SYRIA

CHATHAM HOUSE PAPERS

General Series Editor: William Wallace
Soviet Foreign Policy Programme Director: Alex Pravda

Chatham House Papers are short monographs on current policy problems which have been commissioned by the Royal Institute of International Affairs. In preparing the paper, authors are advised by a study group of experts convened by the RIIA. Publication of the paper by the Institute indicates its standing as an authoritative contribution to the public debate.

The Royal Institute of International Affairs is an independent body which promotes the rigorous study of international questions and does not express opinions of its own. The opinions expressed in this publication are the responsibility of the author.

CHATHAM HOUSE PAPERS

THE
SOVIET UNION
AND SYRIA

THE ASAD YEARS
Efraim Karsh

The Royal Institute of International Affairs

Routledge
London and New York

First published 1988
by Routledge
11 New Fetter Lane, London EC4P 4EE
29 West 35th Street, New York, NY 10001

Reproduced from copy supplied by
Stephen Austin and Sons Ltd, Hertford,
and printed in Great Britain by
Billing & Sons Ltd, Worcester

British Library Cataloguing-in-Publication Data

Karsh, Efraim
  The Soviet Union and Syria.
  (Chatham House papers, ISSN 0143-5795).
  1. Syria. Foreign relations with Soviet Union 2. Soviet Union.
  Foreign relations with Syria
  I. Title II. Series
  327.5691047
ISBN 0-415-03030-7

CONTENTS

For Inari

ACKNOWLEDGMENTS

For their helpful ideas and incisive criticism I am indebted to Ya'acov Ro'i, Yahya Sadowski, Fred Halliday and Helena Cobban. I am especially grateful to Alex Pravda, of the Royal Institute of International Affairs, who helped me in many ways throughout the preparation of this study. A special study group organized by the Royal Institute of International Affairs was very useful. A grant by the Kennan Institute for Advanced Russian Studies also contributed significantly in the later stages of the research. The paper is published under the auspices of the Soviet foreign policy programme funded by the ESRC (grant no. E 00 22 2011).

My toughest critic and source of inspiration has been, as always, my wife, Inari.

Tel Aviv, March 1988   E.K.

1
INTRODUCTION

Alien as it is to Marxist-Leninist ideology, geopolitical thinking has played a focal role in the shaping of Soviet policy towards the Middle East.[1] This is hardly surprising; direct physical contiguity has made the USSR susceptible to the vicissitudes of this volatile area and thus ineluctably interested in its fate. 'The Soviet Union cannot remain indifferent to the situation arising in the Near and Middle East,' read a foreign ministry statement, issued in April 1955 in response to the formation of the Baghdad Pact, 'since ... the USSR is situated very close to these countries'; consequently, the 'establishment of foreign military bases on the territory of the countries of the Near and Middle East has a direct bearing on the security of the USSR.'[2]

A recurrent theme in later Soviet references to the region, the statement provides a striking illustration of the unique position of the Middle East in Soviet political and strategic thinking. To Russia, latterly the Soviet Union, the Middle East is not just another Third World area; it is *the* area, for no reason other than that it is the most volatile part of the Third World immediately adjoining Russian territory, and as such is a vital component of the Russian defence perimeter.[3] The USSR's fundamental interest in the Middle East has therefore been essentially identical with the one held in its immediate European neighbours – Finland, the Baltic countries, the Balkans before World War II, and Central Europe since then – namely, the attainment of a stable and safe frontier in order to minimize potential threats emanating from all these contiguous territories.

1

Stability in this context means both the prevention of external great-power intervention and the preservation of a benevolent local environment. In the case of the Middle East, this interest was further reinforced by Russia's long-standing desire to control the Bosphorus Straits and the Dardanelles in order to provide an outlet for its naval activities in the rest of the world, as well as to block the passage of European warships into the Black Sea.

This geopolitical reality illustrates the fundamental difference between Soviet interest in the Middle East and that of any other great power: whereas Western interest in the Middle East, however vital, is purely circumstantial, Soviet interest is of a structural nature; whereas Western interest in the area is confined to the global level, the USSR has viewed the Middle East in predominantly regional terms. This is not to deny the relevance of global considerations in the making of Soviet policy towards the Middle East, particularly in the postwar system with its intensifying superpower competition for assets in the Third World. Nevertheless, Soviet policy towards this area has revealed far greater constancy and far less dependence on the fluctuations of global events than Western, and in particular American, policies.

Indeed, it is the geographical factor which, by and large, accounts for the lack of Soviet interest in the Arab world until the mid-1950s. Lying further to the south and not contiguous to Soviet territory, these countries were insignificant by comparison with those states immediately adjoining Soviet territory. True, the Arab world has undeniable geostrategic and economic advantages: it occupies a considerable land mass, sits astride waterways of strategic importance and is blessed with abundant deposits of oil. But since the existence of independent Arab states is a relatively new phenomenon, and as the Arab world remained under Western control or influence until the late 1940s or early 1950s, the Soviets were slow to discover the Arab 'revolutionary potential'; instead the USSR focused on the countries of the 'northern tier' – Turkey, Iran and Afghanistan – where its security was more immediately involved and with which its relations had been long and intensive.

Furthermore, there is little doubt that the initial motivation behind the resurgence of Soviet interest in the Arab world in the mid-1950s was directly related to Moscow's preoccupation with the 'northern tier': namely, its desire to undermine the Baghdad Pact which, from the Soviet point of view, constituted a major security threat. Not only did the Pact transform what had been an effective buffer zone in the prewar period into an important link in the worldwide chain of Western containment strategy, but it also meant the extension of NATO's military power to the USSR's backyard, thus turning it into a potential theatre of war.[4]

In these circumstances, Moscow soon began to look for ways and means to stem the West's mounting military power in the Middle East. Unwilling to risk a frontal assault on the USSR's southern neighbours *à la* Stalin, the Soviet leadership sought to contain the Baghdad Pact by adopting an indirect approach: by keeping Afghanistan out of the Pact and trying to pool together those Arab countries opposed to the alliance. These attempts struck a responsive chord in Cairo and Damascus. Considering Iraq the major obstacle to his aspirations to forge a united Arab bloc under Egyptian leadership, President Gamal Abd Al-Nasser sought to dissuade other Arab countries from adhering to the Baghdad Pact; having failed to obtain Western military and economic backing for his goals, Nasser opted for a closer relationship with the USSR.

Syria, by contrast, was driven in the direction of the USSR by mainly defensive considerations. Notorious for its domestic instability and surrounded by hostile countries, Syria's sense of insecurity rose sharply in 1955, following Israel's retaliatory raids on the Arab countries, on the one hand, and Iraqi and Turkish overt threats, accompanied by military shows of force aimed at deflecting Syrian opposition to the Baghdad Pact, on the other. In March 1955 the Soviet Union responded to reported Turkish and Iraqi troop concentrations on the Syrian border by announcing a readiness to extend to Syria 'aid in any form whatsoever for the purpose of safeguarding Syria's independence and sovereignty'.[5] This display of support led shortly to the signing of the first Soviet-Syrian arms deal in the autumn of 1955, and within less than two years Syria is estimated to have purchased more than £100 million worth of Eastern bloc weapons.[6] During the summer and autumn of 1957, the Soviet Union again shielded Damascus from Turkish military pressures, going so far as to threaten that any aggression against Syria 'would not remain limited to this area alone', as well as to dispatch a small naval unit on an official visit to Syria – a show of force hitherto unprecedented in a Middle Eastern, perhaps even Third World, crisis. Finally, the Soviets underscored their support for Syria by signing, on 29 October 1957, a large-scale economic and technical agreement at a total cost of $579 million.[7]

Soviet-Syrian relations underwent a qualitative leap in February 1966, following the rise to power of the left-wing faction of the Ba'th Party. Overthrowing the old leadership of the Ba'th in a bloody coup (the Ba'th had been in power since 8 March 1963), the left-wing regime swiftly moved towards the Soviet Union. In the economic sphere, the Syrian government came to rely almost exclusively on Soviet aid for implementing its various programmes, including the exploitation of Syria's oil resources and the construction of the Euphrates Dam. In the military field, the seriousness of Syria's defeat in the June 1967 War, along with the drying up of Western weapons sources following that war, considerably enhanced the importance of Soviet military aid for the survival of the Ba'th regime. Finally, the USSR utilized both the ideological affinity betweeen the two regimes and Syria's growing hostility towards the West (best illustrated by the severance of diplomatic relations with the major Western powers in the wake of the Six-Day War) in order to develop closer bonds with Damascus. Thus, for example, from the spring of 1966 onwards the Syrian Communist Party, though remaining officially illegal, resumed its activities on the Syrian political scene: its leader, Khaled Bakhdash, was allowed to return to Syria in April 1966 after eight years of exile in Eastern Europe; the communist newspaper *Sawt Al-Arab* received permission to be published, and a communist was appointed Minister of Communications.[8]

Against this backdrop, and notwithstanding occasional frictions with the left-wing Ba'th, the USSR viewed the relationship in highly positive terms and resisted any attempt to rock the fragile edifice of the Syrian political system. Given Syria's record of political instability, the Soviets feared that any change of leadership in Damascus could only be detrimental to their interests. Such apprehensions were exacerbated by the persistent advocacy of a more independent Syrian line by General Hafiz Asad, the Minister of Defence and major contender for the leadership, who was known for his outspoken opposition to Damascus's growing reliance on the USSR.

The intensity of Moscow's distrust of Asad was clearly demonstrated by its reaction to his assumption of *de facto* power in March 1969. Interrupting a vacation in the USSR, the Soviet

Ambassador, Nuridin Mukhidinov, rushed back to Damascus, where he reportedly warned Asad that his complete seizure of power might lead to the withdrawal of Soviet aid and experts from Syria.[9] The Soviet media, for its part, did not conceal its resentment of Asad's attempt to alter the existing balance of forces within the Syrian leadership: 'The internal reaction [in Syria] joined hands with imperialist circles, striving to interrupt the process of socialist transformation,' wrote *Krasnaya Zvezda* on 6 March, 'to weaken Syria's position in its struggle against the Israeli occupiers, to undermine its international position and its relations with the forces of liberation and with the socialist countries.' The Syrian Communist Party was far more outspoken in its criticism. In two statements issued in early and mid-March, the party condemned the developments in Damascus as endangering the unity of the Syrian progressive forces and warned that 'any failure to settle the crisis in accordance with ... the framework of the anti-imperialist progressive policy which Syria adopted on 23 February 1966 ... [might] harm *the existing relations between Syria and the USSR and other friendly socialist bloc countries.*'[10]

Asad responded in kind. In an interview published on 17 March by the British newspaper *The Daily Telegraph*, he did not hesitate to put the blame for his country's domestic and external problems on the USSR. In Asad's view, the 'Soviet-inspired, communist-type regime' in Damascus had reduced Syria from 'the granary of the Middle East' to an impoverished country and served to isolate it from its Arab neighbours. The recovery of Syria from this débâcle required the cessation of 'any interference in a country's internal affairs by another country', as well as the reorganization of the Ba'th Party and the purge of 'extreme leftists in ruling positions'. At the time of this interview, anti-communist feelings were mounting in Damascus, accompanied by reported arrests of hundreds of communists and purges of pro-Soviet elements in the military.

Given this atmosphere of mutual distrust, perhaps even hostility, between the Soviet leadership and Asad, the latter's advent to power in November 1970 certainly did not augur well for Soviet-Syrian relations; indeed, this development gave rise to a wave of hopes and speculations in the West on a dramatic shift in Syria's domestic (i.e., socio-economic) and international orientations.

However, these expectations have been belied by the course of events. Not only has Damascus not broken with Moscow, but it has also developed into the USSR's major Middle Eastern ally: a cosignatory to a bilateral Treaty of Friendship and Cooperation, a recipient of vast military and economic support, and a supplier of political, military and strategic services. Moreover, it is Soviet aid and support which, to a considerable extent, has enabled Asad to transform Syria from a weak country – the object of inter-Arab competition, whose name was synonymous with internal instability – into a regional political and military power whose wishes and interests cannot be ignored.

Broadly speaking, Soviet-Syrian relations from 1970 onwards have undergone two distinct stages, divided by Anwar Sadat's historic visit to Jerusalem in November 1977 and the ensuing Egyptian-Israeli peace process. Until then, the balance sheet of Soviet-Syrian relations clearly tilted in Syria's favour, as the steady Egyptian drift from the Soviet orbit combined with Syria's growing regional standing and influence to increase Moscow's dependence on Damascus. This state of affairs has been fundamentally, though not precipitously, reversed in the period since then, during which President Asad, strengthened in his view that Egypt's desertion of the Arab camp left Syria as the sole active champion of the Arab cause, embarked on an ambitious effort to achieve the 'strategic parity' with Israel that would enable Syria, on its own, to 'regain the usurped Arab rights'. Since the attainment of this objective, as well as the stemming of the mounting tide of domestic opposition to the Asad regime in the late 1970s and early 1980s, required substantial Soviet aid and support, Moscow's leverage over Damascus has increased significantly. This change in fortunes has, in turn, enabled Moscow to consolidate its relations with Damascus while at the same time attempting to broaden its power base in the Arab world, a policy that gained particular momentum under Chernenko and Gorbachev.

The evolution of Soviet-Syrian relations has progressed along three major, interconnected axes, the most important of which is the Arab-Israeli conflict. It is this prolonged and bitter struggle between Arabs and Jews that has created the main avenue for the broadening and deepening of Soviet-Syrian relations, as well as an unsettled bone of contention marring those very relations. The second axis of Soviet-Syrian relations has been the inter-Arab arena, where the Soviet Union has had to manoeuvre between the rivalries and enmities of its radical Arab allies (e.g., Syrian-Iraqi and Syrian-PLO feuds) and its anxiety to keep the relationship with Syria intact, while at the same time broadening Soviet foreign policy beyond the traditional radical camp.

Finally, since the mid-1970s, and particularly since the establishment of a permanent Syrian presence in Lebanon in June 1976, the evolution of Soviet-Syrian relations has become increasingly dependent on the vicissitudes of the Lebanese civil war. Thus, as Lebanon formed the stage for a series of Syrian-Israeli crises, leading ultimately to war, as well as for the power struggle between Damascus and the PLO, it constituted the backdrop against which Soviet-Syrian relations played out some of their most trying moments.

How can this development of Soviet-Syrian relations, from mutual distrust and wariness to proximity and convergence, be explained? What goals and motivations have shaped the evolution of Soviet policy towards Syria during the Asad era? What means and techniques have been used in pursuit of these goals? These are the major questions addressed in this study.

2
COOPERATION AND CONFLICT

The formative years

Fully aware of his 'anti-Soviet' reputation, Asad made it one of his immediate goals following his accession to power on 13 November 1970 to reassure the USSR of Syria's future course. As well as including two communists in the new government, the newly established Provisional Regional Command of the Ba'th Party released a statement announcing its continued adherence to the guidelines set by 'the Party's congresses and theories', and its intention to 'develop relations with the socialist camp, particularly with the friendly USSR'.[1]

Three months later, in February 1971, another move was made to consolidate Soviet-Syrian relations when Asad paid his first official visit to the USSR as head of state. Despite the surfacing of certain differences, in particular Syria's rejection of Security Council Resolution 242 as a basis for an Arab-Israeli settlement, the visit completely dispelled any remaining hopes in the West of a reversal in Syria's foreign policy orientation. Rather, it underlined the two parties' keen interest in continuing their special relationship and opened an era of close Soviet-Syrian cooperation which was to last – though not without occasional differences – until the outbreak of the October 1973 War.[2]

Already in 1971, the volume of Soviet and East European economic activity in Syria, as well as the scope of bilateral exchanges of delegations, grew significantly; the spring and the summer of 1971 also witnessed the beginning of a steady flow of Soviet arms to Syria. In February 1972 an agreement on Soviet economic and technical support to Syria was signed, to be followed three months later by an arms deal signed during a visit to Damascus by the Soviet Minister of Defence, Andrei Grechko. Soviet-Syrian military relations were significantly upgraded later in the year following the conclusion of two additional arms deals: a $700 million deal signed during Asad's second visit to Moscow, on 5–8 July 1972, and a follow-up agreement concluded during a Moscow visit in December by the Syrian Minister of Defence, Mustafa Tlas.[3]

Coming at a time when the USSR was using delaying tactics in its arms supplies to Egypt in order to prevent President Anwar Sadat from going to war, the growing Soviet military support to Syria seems, on the face of it, inexplicable. After all, it was Sadat, rather than Asad, who accepted United Nations Resolution 242 and who participated in the Jarring peace initiative; it was Sadat who institutionalized his country's relations with the USSR in the form of a bilateral treaty, whereas Asad remained resistant to repeated Soviet pleas to sign such an agreement.[4] Moreover, Sadat's decision to abandon the search for a political solution in favour of the military option did not essentially differ from Asad's position at the time, which rejected a peaceful settlement of the Arab-Israeli conflict. If the Soviets were unequivocally opposed to the outbreak of another war in the Middle East, as indeed they were, why did they not stop supplying the most outspoken proponent of the military option: Asad?[5]

This apparent contradiction in Soviet behaviour appears to have derived from four interconnected considerations. In the first place, the USSR assessed, and not unjustifiably, that notwithstanding Asad's vocal advocacy of the military option, he would not go to war without Egypt, whereas Sadat, on the other hand, was ready to launch a war on his own, should the need arise. Hence, viewing the decision on war to be essentially an Egyptian one, the USSR focused its pressures upon Cairo and refrained from translating its fundamental differences with Syria into military sanctions. Second, despite the formal unification of the Syrian and Egyptian commands following the establishment of the Egyptian-Syrian-Libyan federation in April 1971, it was only in April 1973 that Syria joined the projected Egyptian campaign.[6] Third, the tranquillity along the

Egyptian-Israeli border in the wake of the ceasefire agreement of August 1970, as contrasted with the ongoing low-intensity hostilities between Israel and Syria, which considerably increased the latter's need for military support, enabled the USSR to distinguish between the military aid to Syria and that to Egypt.

Finally, and perhaps most importantly, the intensification of Soviet-Syrian relations from 1971 onwards reflected Moscow's awareness of its precarious position in Egypt (in May 1971 Sadat removed Ali Sabri, the USSR's staunchest supporter within the Egyptian leadership, from power, eventually bringing him and his followers to trial on charges of conspiring against the state) and its intention to prepare an alternative, however partial, to Egypt. This intention gained momentum after the expulsion of about 15,000 Soviet military personnel from Egypt in July 1972.[7]

This decoupling of Soviet policy between Syria and Egypt was generously rewarded by Damascus. Not only did Asad refrain from exploiting the deterioration in Soviet-Egyptian relations in order to extract benefits from the USSR, but he toiled to mend the rift between Moscow and Cairo. As early as 10 July 1972, on the way home from the USSR, Asad stopped in Cairo, where he questioned the prudence of Sadat's decision.[8] In the following months, Asad was reported to have conveyed messages between Egypt and the USSR in an attempt to smooth over differences between the two countries, and in late September he paid a two-day unofficial visit to Moscow which apparently led to the return of the Soviet and Egyptian ambassadors to their respective capitals after an absence of two months.

Furthermore, though not subjected to heavy Soviet pressures, and perhaps for this very reason, Asad proved rather receptive to the USSR and its interests. The most striking illustration of this responsiveness was afforded in May 1973 when, following a Soviet request made during his secret visit to Moscow, he succeeded in persuading Sadat not to go to war before the convening of the Brezhnev-Nixon summit in June.[9]

However impressive, the Soviet success in forestalling the war in May 1973 proved to be short-lived. Despite Brezhnev's dramatic efforts during the June summit, the Soviet leader failed to convey to his American counterparts the inflammability of the Middle East situation: considering Brezhnev's warnings of the impending war to be no more than 'psychological warfare', Nixon and Kissinger refused to cooperate with Moscow in arranging a peace settlement or to apply pressure on Israel to moderate its position.[10]

The outcome of the summit was received by Asad with deep disappointment. After all, it was he who, despite his public commitment to the military option, had acquiesced in the Soviet request to exhaust the political process. The USSR's failure to live up to Asad's expectations was therefore bound to incur a measure of Syrian criticism. 'The Soviet-American accord comes at the expense of the weak and vanquished peoples, above all our people,' wrote *Al-Ba'th* on 25 June; 'even if the whole world breathes the fragrance of accord, the fact that our people has the right to their land and dignity cannot be changed.' Asad's loss of faith in Moscow's ability to promote the Arab cause by peaceful means was further illustrated by his reported rejection of a Soviet request for restraint, forwarded to him by a member of the Politburo, Andrei Kirilenko, who was on a visit to Damascus in July 1973.[11]

Interestingly enough, Asad's deep frustration over the Soviet failure to advance the Arab cause, and his consequent decision to go to war in October, did not shake the overall edifice of Soviet-Syrian relations. As long as Soviet military equipment kept on pouring into Syria, Asad did not see much point in clashing with the USSR. The Soviets, for their part, aware of no more than the general Arab intention to launch a war on the earliest possible occasion (Sadat informed the Soviet ambassador of the impending attack on 3 October and Asad followed suit a day later), and in the light of their shaky position in Egypt, were less than enthusiastic to jeopardize their relationship with Syria. Accordingly, apart from unconfirmed reports of restrictions on the activities of Soviet advisers deployed within the Syrian armed forces, Soviet-Syrian relations continued unhindered.

The October 1973 War

To the USSR, the October 1973 War was the wrong war at the wrong time, for many reasons. These ranged from apprehensions that a Middle Eastern war might hamper the course of detente, to which the USSR was then committed, all the way to the fear that such a conflict could lead the USSR's Arab allies to conclude that the road to regaining their lost territories passed through the United States – the only power capable of forcing concessions on Israel.

Hence, not only did the USSR try to prevent the outbreak of hostilities, but it also sought to contain the war at its various stages; this anxiety to terminate hostilities was, however, bound to antagonize Moscow's two Arab allies.

The Soviet clash with Egypt over the ceasefire issue took place within a few hours of the outbreak of hostilities, when the Soviet Ambassador to Egypt, Sergei Vinogradov, unsuccessfully pressed Sadat to accept what he claimed to be a Syrian-proposed ceasefire.[12] The Soviet encounter with Syria over the same issue occurred towards the end of the war, when a joint Soviet-American ceasefire proposal was approved on 22 October by a special session of the Security Council as Resolution 338. Calling upon the belligerents to terminate military hostilities within twelve hours and to start negotiations 'under appropriate auspices' immediately thereafter for the implementation of Resolution 242 and the establishment of 'a just and durable peace in the Middle East', Resolution 338 was not welcomed by Damascus. For one thing, Syria's complete exclusion from the US-Soviet negotiations on the ceasefire agreement was perceived by Asad as a personal and national humiliation.[13] Also, since Israel's major effort at the time was directed against Egypt, Asad did not have any sense of urgency about the need for a ceasefire. Instead he apparently sought to exploit this favourable conjuncture in order to launch a counter-attack with Iraq.[14] Moreover, the cessation of hostilities on 22 October would have saved the Egyptian Third Army, deployed on the eastern side of the Suez Canal, thereby leaving Egypt with some visible territorial gains. Such an eventuality would only have highlighted Syria's failure to achieve similar successes and, as a consequence, might have eroded Asad's domestic power base. Finally, the ceasefire resolution was based on Security Council Resolution 242 of 22 November 1967, to which Syria, at the time, was adamantly opposed; its acceptance, therefore, could be interpreted as a sign of weakness on Asad's part. Given these clear disadvantages, it was only natural that Asad should choose to ignore the ceasefire resolution completely; it took two more days of fighting and another Security Council resolution, Resolution 339, to convince him to halt fire and accept Resolutions 338 and 339.

Despite its anxiety to contain the war, the USSR could not afford to remain aloof and watch its Arab allies suffer yet another military defeat by Israel. Indeed, the October War precipitated the first massive Soviet resupply effort to a Third World belligerent in the course of full hostilities. Carried out simultaneously by sea and air on an unprecedented scale, it began a day after the onset of hostilities: on 7 October the first ships left Odessa, arriving in Syria three days later. By the end of the war, the USSR had airlifted to Syria some 4,360 tons of war *matériel*, while some 38,210 tons were sent by sea.[15]

As a rule, the sea- and airlift did not suffer direct attacks by the Israeli army; however, there were a few exceptions. Several Soviet transport aircraft were destroyed on the ground during the airlift, and a merchant ship, *Ilya Mechnikov*, was accidentally sunk in the port of Tartus on 12 October by Israeli missiles that were being fired at Syrian boats.[16]

Moscow's reaction to the sinking of the merchant vessel was prompt and angry. On 12 October, only a few hours after the incident, the Soviet news agency, *Tass*, issued its first warning to Israel: 'The USSR cannot regard indifferently the criminal actions of the Israeli military, as a result of which there are victims also among Soviet citizens.' Thus Israel must 'strictly observe . . . the international laws, including those regarding the freedom of navigation. The continuation of criminal acts by Israel will lead to grave consequences to Israel itself.'

The flow of arms into Syria was paralleled by the wide range of activities performed by the Soviet advisory mission, which was deployed within the Syrian armed forces. Plain clothes Soviet air force technicians reassembled the fighter aircraft that were shipped to Syria in the sea- and airlift; Soviet advisers drove tanks from Latakia and Tartus to Damascus; and Soviet engineers repaired military equipment damaged in the fighting. Soviet advisers held Syrian command posts at every level, from battalion up. However, they did not occupy frontline positions.[17]

Soviet support for Syria during the war was not confined to arms shipments and advisory assistance but was also manifested in supportive activities performed by regular Soviet units. About a week after the outbreak of hostilities, air defence missile units under exclusive Soviet operation and control were deployed at Latakia and in the Damascus area, presumably to protect the sea- and airlift.[18] The Mediterranean Squadron, for its part, conducted surveillance activities against the Sixth Fleet, as well as naval operations in support of the Arab war effort. These included intelligence-gathering by two ships, operating off the Israeli coast, and the protection of the sea- and airlift. On 13 October, a day after the sinking of the *Ilya Mechnikov*, Soviet warships appeared to the north and east of Cyprus with the clear aim of providing some measure of protection for Soviet merchant ships carrying arms to Syria. These ships remained near the Syrian coast until the end of hostilities, departing some time between 24 and 26 October.[19]

The October War also witnessed two Soviet threats to dispatch ground forces to the combat zone. The second – and better known – was made on 24 October, when the Soviet Union announced that it would send troops to Egypt if Israel did not immediately halt its advance. The first was related to events on the Syrian front.

On 10 October, after the recapture of the Golan Heights by Israel, the USSR placed at least three of its seven airborne divisions on advanced alert.[20] Three days later, when Israeli troops crossed the 'purple line' and began advancing towards Damascus, Moscow warned Israel through Kissinger that Soviet airborne forces were on the alert to move to the defence of Damascus.[21] These indirect warnings were paralleled by *unconfirmed* reports indicating that the advanced staff of a Soviet airborne division had been settled in Syrian headquarters at Qatana, outside Damascus.[22]

It is difficult to assess the impact of the Soviet threat on Israel's decision to avoid further thrusts into Syria; there were other weighty military and political considerations which may well have been decisive in themselves. Nonetheless, according to a leading Israeli analyst, 'when to these considerations were added the Soviet interest in the security of Damascus and the Soviet threats, it was obviously not in Israel's interest to advance beyond a point from which Damascus could be threatened by Israeli artillery fire.'[23]

Disengagement
However undesirable in itself, the October War opened the way for a potentially positive development from the Soviet point of view: it broke the existing political stalemate and set in train a process of negotiation between Israel and its Arab neighbours which had long been advocated by the USSR. Accordingly, Moscow responded very favourably to the (reluctant) Syrian acceptance of Resolution 338, which implied Syria's recognition, however qualified, of Resolution 242. Anxious to establish an Arab-Israeli settlement through an

international peace conference, under the auspices of the United Nations and co-chaired by the two superpowers, the Soviets ignored the angry words accompanying the Syrian ceasefire decision and interpreted Asad's recognition of Resolution 242 as implying Syria's possible participation in such a conference. Throughout November and December 1973 the USSR went to great lengths to highlight to Damascus time and again the importance of the political settlement of the Arab-Israeli conflict by means of an international conference. The main Soviet argument was that as a result of several factors (such as increased Soviet-American cooperation, Arab unity, the destruction of the myth of Israel's military superiority), the 'current political atmosphere was more suitable than at any other time for the establishment of justice and peace in the Middle East';[24] any failure to exploit this favourable conjuncture to its fullest would, therefore, be a historical mistake. The Soviet attempts at persuasion were of no avail. On 18 December 1973, following a heated debate within the Syrian leadership, Damascus officially announced its decision not to participate in the Geneva conference.

Dismayed as they were with the Syrian decision, the Soviets did not exert pressures on Asad to make him reconsider his position. On the contrary. Considering the convening of the Geneva conference on 21–22 December 1973 as a major achievement in its own right, and reluctant to risk a confrontation with Damascus at a time when Egypt was distancing itself from the USSR, Moscow chose to put the blame for Syria's absence on the Israeli 'tactics of procrastination'. According to the Soviets, Syria's non-participation in Geneva was motivated neither by the country's opposition to the holding of the conference nor by its rejection of a political settlement; rather it reflected Syria's reluctance to play into Israel's hands. In fact, there was no 'essential difference between the attitude of Syria and that of Egypt, Jordan and the other Arab countries towards the question of a Middle East settlement'.[25]

The vocal Soviet defence of the Syrian position notwithstanding, Moscow's growing impatience with Damascus's intransigence manifested itself, after the conclusion of the Egyptian-Israeli disengagement agreement of 18 January 1974, in pressures on Damascus (reportedly through withholding arms supplies) to provide Israel with a list of prisoners of war, which would pave the way for Syrian-Israeli talks on disengagement under the auspices of the Geneva conference.[26] These pressures were reinforced, on 30 January, by an

15

article in *Pravda* signed by 'Observer' – a pseudonym usually recognized as representing the policy positions of the Politburo. Criticizing Syria indirectly for its absence from Geneva, the article argued that 'the question of the return of Syrian territories is just as acute as the question of the return of all the Arab lands occupied by Israel. The problem of the disengagement of troops as the first step to resolve the question of the return of these territories also directly concerns Syria.'

Soviet pressure on Syria, especially the arms supply cutback, indicated the intensity of Moscow's interest in the reconvening of Geneva. The possibility of yet another stalemate in the Middle East, and of Syria's following the Egyptian example and joining the American-sponsored negotiations process outside the Geneva framework, seemed alarming enough to make the USSR risk a crisis with Syria – at a time when its relations with Egypt were further deteriorating. It was not long, however, before the Soviet policy backfired: by February 1974, ignoring the Geneva forum completely, Asad headed towards a disengagement agreement with Israel under American auspices. Furthermore, on 5 February, by way of consolidating his bargaining position during the negotiations process, he launched a war of attrition against Israel on the Golan Heights. Faced once again with the spectre of exclusion from the political process (the USSR was not brought into the picture during the Egyptian-Israeli disengagement talks), the Soviets moved quickly. In two visits to Damascus – on 27–28 February and 4–7 March 1974 – the Soviet Foreign Minister, Andrei Gromyko, tried to highlight to the Syrian leadership the importance of cooperation with the USSR. He stressed that any agreement accomplished and guaranteed unilaterally by the United States was doomed to fail; it was in Syria's best interest, therefore, to strive for an accord worked out jointly and guaranteed by both superpowers within the framework of the Geneva conference. Gromyko's arguments fell on deaf ears. Not only did the Syrians reject his suggestion to reconvene the Geneva plenum,[27] but he found himself accommodating their position on several issues. While emphasizing the importance of Soviet participation in the Middle East peace process 'at all stages', as well as the 'usefulness of regular [bilateral] contacts at all levels', the joint communiqué issued at the end of Gromyko's second visit (7 March) carried no mention of the Geneva conference. A no less important Soviet gesture towards Damascus was the reference to Syria's

16

'legitimate, inalienable right to use all *effective means* for the liberation of its occupied lands' – the first official Soviet support for Syria's war of attrition. Finally, the communiqué contained a Soviet pledge to continue 'all-round support' to Syria, particularly in the economic and military fields;[28] the arms embargo was lifted within a fortnight of Gromyko's visit.

The Soviet eagerness to court Syria was further demonstrated a month later, during Asad's official visit to Moscow on 11–16 April 1974. Coming against the background of intensifying Syrian-American contacts and an accelerated deterioration in Soviet-Egyptian relations, Asad's visit proved very successful from the Syrian point of view. Apart from securing reconfirmed support for the war of attrition (the joint communiqué reiterated the Soviet pledge to consolidate Syria's 'defence capacity, and its lawful, inalienable right to use all effective means for liberating its occupied territories'),[29] the visit produced a whole host of bilateral agreements in several fields: from inter-party relations through cultural and technical cooperation to trade exchange. Most important were the signing of a long-term economic agreement (which reportedly stipulated, among other things, a twelve-year moratorium on Syria's military debt)[30] and the conclusion of a large-scale arms deal providing for the delivery of some hundred tanks (most of them T-62s) and surface-to-air missiles, as well as some major weapons systems, such as SCUD-B surface-to-surface missiles and MiG-23 aircraft, which until then had not been supplied to Syria.[31]

The Soviet balance sheet was more equivocal but still rather satisfactory. True, neither the emphasis laid by Asad during the visit on the importance of Soviet participation in the negotiations nor his promise of regular consultations with the USSR was of any practical value, since Syria (and the United States) had no intention of allowing Moscow to play a real role in the final stage of the negotiations, begun in May 1974. Yet, in contrast with the complete exclusion of the USSR from the Egyptian-Israeli disengagement talks, both Damascus and Washington were prepared to give the Soviets an appearance of participation in the negotiations process. Thus, the decision to have the disengagement agreement signed in Geneva constituted a clear American, and much more so Syrian, gesture to the Soviet Union. Similarly, a joint Soviet-Syrian statement issued on 29 May, at the end of Gromyko's visit to Damascus and a few hours before the announcement of the Syrian-Israeli

17

disengagement agreement, underlined the importance of Soviet participation in every stage of a political settlement. Reiterating the Soviet view that a separation of forces was merely 'a first step and an indivisible part of the comprehensive solution', the communiqué went on to stress the urgency of continuing the quest for an overall settlement.[32]

These shows of goodwill appear to have satisfied the Soviets. Reassured about Syrian intentions and contented with the image of participation they had obtained, they did not see much point in clashing with Syria or the United States, which linked Soviet acquiescence in its Middle Eastern initiative with the entire structure of detente. Therefore, instead of trying to undermine Kissinger's mediation efforts, or even to play an active role in the final stage of the negotiations, they preferred to focus on being *seen* to be actively participating in all stages of the talks.[33]

That Moscow was less interested in playing a real role in the discussions than in creating such an impression was evident not only from the pattern of two additional visits paid by Gromyko to Syria in May, at a stage when the Soviet Union could hardly keep a close watch on, let alone engage in, the delicate negotiations process, but also from the tone of Brezhnev's congratulatory message to Asad on 30 May, a day before the signing of the agreement. In it he expressed satisfaction with the achievement of the agreement, which 'set the beginning of the liberation of Syrian territory occupied by the Israeli invaders' and was the result of close Soviet-Syrian cooperation.[34]

Closing the ranks

Despite the satisfactory outcome of the two disengagement agreements, the USSR remained concerned about the future course of the political process in the Middle East. Viewing these agreements both as a means to defuse potential military dangers and as a prelude to a comprehensive settlement, Moscow had nothing against their actual signing. However, the process through which they had been reached was far more worrying for the Soviets, since it unequivocally exposed the American advantage over the USSR as a peacebroker, thus entailing the risk of further erosion of Soviet standing in the region. The sole way to bridge this gap between ends and means, between the USSR's interest in the continuation of the political process and its reluctance to see a *Pax Americana* in the Middle East, lay through the reconvening of the Geneva conference. Only by transforming the evolving Arab-Israeli dialogue into a multilateral process could the Soviets hope to compensate for their inherent inferiority *vis-à-vis* the United States on the bilateral level, without at the same time tarnishing detente.

The need to reconvene Geneva became far more pressing from Moscow's point of view in the light of the fact that not only did the major pillar of Soviet Middle Eastern policy, namely Egypt, collapse in the aftermath of the October War, but Syria, too, was showing alarming signs. Following the conclusion of the disengagement agreement with Israel, Asad indicated on several occasions, though without distancing himself from the USSR, his interest in fostering the newly established Syrian-American cooperation.[35] Syria's forthcoming approach to the United States was further illustrated by a series of favourable references on the part of leading Syrian politicians to the American role in the negotiations process,[36] and even more by the warm reception for President Nixon during his visit to Syria on 15–16 June 1974. The visit produced a number of concrete results, including the restoration of diplomatic relations (broken off in 1967 following the Six-Day War) and an American promise of economic aid totalling $100 million.[37]

Equally worrying from the Soviet standpoint was Syria's economic, and to a lesser extent military, 'openness' to Western Europe. The decision of the Syrian government on 13 March 1974 to lift restrictions on the movement of private capital in and out of Syria as well as to permit the private sector to sign loan agreements with foreign investors, together with declarations by prominent Syrian figures, including Asad himself, about the need for a greater measure of economic interaction with the West, combined to increase Soviet concern over Syria's future course.[38] The Soviets must also have been unhappy about Syria's interest, however limited, in purchasing sophisticated weapons systems (e.g., electronic warfare) from France and Britain.[39]

To Moscow's great relief the Syrian-American 'honeymoon' ended quickly. Already in the early summer of 1974 Syria realized, to its dismay, that it did not figure high on the American list of priorities. Either because of its eagerness to exploit the Egyptian opening to the full, or because of the difficulties involved in reaching another agreement on the Golan Heights, the US administration decided to leave Syria aside, at least for some time, and to concentrate on achieving an Egyptian-Israeli agreement, to be followed, if possible, by a Jordanian-Israeli one.[40] In these circumstances and in the light of the growing differences between Egypt and Syria, a convergence of Soviet-Syrian interests took place. By way of shoring up Syria's relations with the Soviet Union, Asad adopted, for the first time, during talks with Brezhnev in Moscow on 26–27 September 1974, the Soviet position on the need for the immediate reconvening of the Geneva conference. The Soviet leader, for his part, anxious to cement the tentative *rapprochement* with Syria, reciprocated this concession by promising his guest fresh military supplies as well as additional economic aid.[41]

Soviet-Syrian cooperation grew during the autumn of 1974 as Syria increasingly identified itself with the Soviet demand to reactivate Geneva;[42] this process culminated in the joint communiqué, issued following Gromyko's visit to Damascus in February 1975, which called for the immediate resumption of Geneva by February or early March 1975 at the latest.[43] By that time, Syria had apparently developed into the pivot of Soviet Middle Eastern policy. However interested in improving their shaky position in Egypt and however pleased with Sadat's occasional gestures in late 1974, the Soviets remained wary of the Egyptian president; they rejected his requests for arms and economic aid and focused their efforts on Syria, rendering it extensive political, military and economic support (e.g., deferral of debts).[44] Indeed, Brezhnev's speech in Kishinev on 11 October 1974 ranked Syria first, before Egypt and Iraq, on the list of Middle East countries maintaining 'friendly cooperation' with the Soviet Union.[45] This trend also found a clear echo in the Soviet press. Writing in *Za Rubezhom* in late February 1975, Igor Belayev, a leading commentator on Middle Eastern affairs, praised Syria's successful handling of its complex domestic and foreign affairs, while emphasizing the growing internal, in particular economic, problems in Egypt.[46] Similarly, a *Kommunist* article by Lev Tolkunov, chief editor of *Izvestiya*, cited Soviet-Syrian collaboration as a model for other countries. Implying thinly veiled criticism of the Egyptian approach, Tolkunov argued that 'when the Arab states consistently act together with the Soviet Union in the struggle for their rights, then the Israeli aggressors' room for manoeuvre is reduced, and they are forced into concessions. When the opposite is the case, the positions of the invader, as a rule, become tougher.'[47]

While previous Soviet references to collaboration with Syria reflected, by and large, wishful thinking rather than an existing reality, Tolkunov's analysis was based on far more solid ground. In contrast with his completely independent conduct during the disengagement talks, in late 1974 Asad cooperated actively with the USSR in obstructing Kissinger's attempts to revive the American 'step-by-step' policy. Thus during three visits to Damascus – on 11 and 14 October and on 7 November – Kissinger was faced with a unified Soviet-Syrian rejection of any partial arrangements. Amidst a wave of Soviet and Syrian public calls for the reconvening of Geneva, Kissinger held several meetings with Asad only to learn about Damascus's 'firm stand towards the question of peace in the Middle East'.[48] According to some reports, not only did Asad dismiss out of hand Kissinger's insinuations that Israel might attack Syria unless the latter made some steps in the direction of negotiations, but he also made the renewal of the United Nations Disengagement Observers Force (UNDOF) mandate after 30 November conditional on some concrete measures, such as a further Israeli withdrawal on the Golan Heights, or at least the reconvening of Geneva. Moreover, Asad was reported to have told Kissinger that in the event of another separate Israeli-Egyptian agreement, Syria would have no choice but to resort to arms in order to force Israel to make territorial concessions.[49]

Asad's 'firm position' was accompanied by a series of Syrian activities in the inter-Arab arena, aimed at frustrating any progress towards an American-inspired arrangement. Most notably, a 'coordination conference' in Cairo on 22 September 1974 between Egypt, Syria and the PLO adopted the Syrian-Soviet approach, namely rejection of any partial settlement and recognition of the PLO as the sole representative of the Palestinian people. These decisions, which were reconfirmed by the Arab League summit conference in Rabat (26–29 October 1974), together with the appearance of the PLO leader, Yasser Arafat, at the UN General Assembly in November 1974, constituted a major advance for the Soviet-Syrian coalition: they blocked the possibility of a separate Israeli-Jordanian agreement and frustrated, at least temporarily, American efforts to bring about a second Egyptian-Israeli agreement. During the visit of the Egyptian Foreign Minister, Ismail Fahmi, to Moscow in mid-October, the USSR and Egypt affirmed their support for the reconvening of Geneva with the participation of the PLO.

The consolidated Soviet-Syrian relationship was put to a severe test in early 1975 as a result of a new American initiative to engineer a second separate Egyptian-Israeli agreement. Encouraged by the success of their joint strategy in late 1974 and unwilling to see the United States regaining the leading role in the Middle East, the Soviets sought to pre-empt the new American initiative by dispatching Andrei Gromyko to Damascus and Cairo in early February, a week before the opening of a new stage of Kissinger's 'shuttle diplomacy'. When this visit failed to prevent Sadat from embarking on a new round of American-sponsored negotiations with Israel, the USSR and Syria coordinated their moves in an attempt to forestall the renewed Egyptian-Israeli dialogue. As well as running an aggressive propaganda campaign in both the Soviet and the Syrian media against partial settlements, or 'half-way measures', as they were called,[50] Syria sought to consolidate its relations with both the PLO and Jordan, in order to bring these sworn rivals closer together under Syrian leadership, thus increasing Egypt's isolation in the Arab world. In a brilliant diplomatic move on 7 March, Asad announced Syria's willingness to unify its political leadership as well as military command with that of the PLO; with the PLO's acceptance of this invitation a week later, Syria became identified with the Palestinian cause.

Syria's cooperation with Jordan began in late 1973, when Jordan represented Syrian interests at the Geneva conference, and intensified in late 1974, as the two countries were united in their rejection of the Egyptian search for a separate deal with Israel. The growing Syrian-Jordanian collaboration was also motivated by the shared fear that in the case of another Syrian-Israeli war, the main Israeli thrust against Syria would push through the northwestern part of Jordan rather than the heavily fortified Golan Heights. Consequently, in mid-December 1974 the two leaderships apparently reached an understanding on a joint military policy *vis-à-vis* Israel, to be followed by a far-reaching agreement on economic and technical cooperation in early March 1975.[51] The Soviets, for their part, sought to encourage the growing Syrian-Jordanian amity by sending Vladimir Vinogradov, the Soviet representative in Geneva, for talks with King Hussein in mid-March.[52]

It is difficult to determine the weight of the Soviet-Syrian strategy in the overall balance of factors leading to the collapse of Kissinger's mediation attempts on 22 March 1975. Yet there is little doubt that the very establishment of the united Syrian-Jordanian-Palestinian front under Soviet blessing highlighted Sadat's isolation in the Arab world, thereby reducing his room for manoeuvre and preventing him from displaying flexibility towards Israel. The Israeli leadership, at the same time, constrained by domestic political factors (e.g., opposition to compromises, the delicate balance of power between Premier Rabin and Defence Minister Peres) and uncertain about the possible implications of unfavourable regional developments (e.g., the Iraqi-Iranian agreement of March 1975), was reluctant to acquiesce in Sadat's demand for a withdrawal from strategic Sinai passes and from the Abu Rodeis oilfields as long as the Egyptian president did not agree to end the state of belligerence between the two countries. And since Sadat felt unable to do so, an impasse was created.[53]

But whatever the reasons for the failure of Kissinger's mission, Syria and the USSR perceived this development as both an outcome of their 'principled' policy and an indication that Geneva constituted the most effective means for overcoming Israeli intransigence. Subsequently, in the summer of 1975, when the United States resumed its efforts to mediate in an Egyptian-Israeli agreement, Asad rejected several American attempts to convince Syria to join the step-by-step diplomacy. Instead he chose to adhere to the same strategy which, in his view, had obstructed the Egyptian-Israeli negotiations in March: namely, cooperation with the Soviet Union in discrediting the American policy, on the one hand,[54] and attempts to increase Egypt's isolation in the Arab world by fostering the evolving framework of cooperation with Jordan, as well as by seeking to mitigate Syrian-Iraqi hostility, on the other. Nevertheless, unlike March 1975, neither the Soviet-Syrian propaganda campaign nor Egypt's isolation prevented the 'step-by-step policy' from culminating in a three-year Egyptian-Israeli disengagement agreement in late August 1975.

For the Soviet Union the signing of the second disengagement agreement was largely a negative development. For one, it signified the *de facto* termination of almost two decades of close Soviet-Egyptian alignment; the *de jure* breaking-point of this relationship took place a few months later in March 1976, with Egypt's unilateral abrogation of the 1971 Treaty of Friendship and Cooperation with the USSR. Second, not only did the agreement – like its predecessor – depict the United States as the only power capable of forcing Israel into territorial concessions, but it also established the American military presence in the region in the form of both US observation devices operated by American personnel and the establishment of procurement relations between Egypt and the United States. Finally, the failure of the Soviet-Syrian effort to forestall the agreement exposed Moscow's limited control over regional developments and its consequent need to lean on local actors in defence of Soviet interests: it was Syria, rather than the Soviet Union, which spearheaded the struggle against a separate Egyptian-Israeli deal, starting with the initiation of the Rabat decisions in October 1974 and ending with the formation of an eastern front to counterbalance Egypt's 'desertion' from the Arab fold. All the Soviets could, and did in effect, do was to strengthen Syria in its vehement rejection of the Egyptian policy and to render it the necessary political, military and propaganda backing.

Yet the Egyptian-Israeli agreement had a major advantage from the Soviet point of view in that it drove Syria even closer to the USSR. Though clearly gaining a higher status in the Arab world as a result of Egypt's growing isolation, Asad perceived Sadat's move both as a betrayal of the Arab cause and as a personal offence by a comrade-in-arms. In Asad's view, the removal of Egypt from the Arab-Israeli conflict upset the regional balance of power in favour of Israel and left Syria alone, as 'an orphan', in the frontline of the Arab struggle.[55] Wary of King Hussein, distrustful of the Iraqi leadership, concerned over the domestic deterioration in Lebanon, Asad came gradually to the conclusion that by way of restoring the strategic balance Syria had to rely primarily, though not exclusively, on its intrinsic resources. This meant both an uncompromising political posture on the issue of a partial settlement and a major drive to enhance Syria's military potential so as to enable it to lead the Arab campaign and, if necessary, to fight Israel on its own.[56]

Asad's strategic conception, first manifested in September 1975, when Syria rejected yet another American offer to negotiate a partial agreement with Israel,[57] largely coincided with the USSR's regional interests. Syria's categorical rejection of a partial settlement with Israel in effect dealt a mortal blow to the American shuttle diplomacy. Moreover, the increased Syrian emphasis on military expansion heralded a further intensification of Soviet-Syrian military relations. Nevertheless, Asad was quick to present the Soviets with a bill for his policy. In a two-day working visit to Moscow, on

9–10 October 1975, which produced a large-scale arms deal, he clarified to the Soviet leaders that Syria's rejection of American overtures did not mean automatic support for the Geneva option. Instead of investing futile efforts in reactivating Geneva, the Syrian leader requested Soviet support for his scheme to advance the Palestinian cause by linking the extension of the UNDOF mandate on the Golan Heights with the amendment of Security Council Resolution 242.[58]

The Syrian plan to amend Resolution 242 put Moscow between the hammer and the anvil. After all, this resolution had constituted the general framework for consecutive Soviet peace plans since 1967 and, by extension, the basis for the Geneva conference; its amendment would necessitate a fundamental reorientation in the Soviet position. Still, an objection to the Syrian initiative might create an open rift between the USSR and its two major Middle Eastern allies, Syria and the PLO, at a time when Soviet-Egyptian relations were at a low ebb. Soviet distress was compounded by the fact that Syria was supporting its initiative with an escalation of tension along its border with Israel.

As on previous occasions, it was the United States that took the Soviets out of their predicament. Faced with unequivocal American opposition to his initiative, Asad abandoned the plan to amend Resolution 242, reducing the price for the extension of the UNDOF mandate to the demand that the Security Council should reconvene in January 1976 for a discussion on the Middle East with the participation of the PLO. Adopted by the Security Council on 30 November 1975, the Syrian compromise proposal was received in Moscow with much relief: it removed a potential obstacle in Soviet-Syrian relations and constituted a diplomatic gain for the PLO and a political setback for Israel. Moreover, when the Security Council discussion did, in fact, take place, on 12–26 January 1976, Moscow managed to appear as the champion of the Palestinian cause and to embarrass the United States by bringing it to veto a draft resolution which affirmed the Palestinians' right to self-determination and statehood and called for a complete Israeli withdrawal from the Arab lands occupied in 1967. In any event, the uneasiness in Soviet-Syrian relations attending Syria's initiative to amend Resolution 242 turned out to be a passing episode; it was not long before the Lebanese question came to overshadow all other aspects of the bilateral relationship.

3
CRISIS OVER LEBANON

To Syria, Lebanon has never been just another neighbouring country. It is an integral and indivisible part of 'Greater Syria',[1] torn away unjustifiably by France in the wake of World War I; illustrative of this indivisibility is the fact that no formal diplomatic ties have ever existed between the two countries. As Asad declared:

> Throughout history, Syria and Lebanon have been one country and one people with so many genuine interests binding them in common. This must be well realized by everybody. Genuine joint interests, a genuine joint security also resulted. Close kinship in the two countries has also resulted ... It is difficult to draw a line between Lebanon's security in its broad sense and Syria's security.[2]

Given this outlook, Syria followed with utmost alarm the eruption of civil war in Lebanon in April 1975, which threatened to destroy the country's delicate social, political and religious balance. For Syria the Lebanese events were direct results of an 'imperialist-Zionist' plot, whose goals ranged from the desire to 'cover up the Sinai agreement' by creating a new regional crisis, to the intention 'to embroil and strike at the Resistance and liquidate its camps,' thus forcing Syria to divert its resources from the struggle against Israel, to the wish 'to bring about the partition of Lebanon'.[3]

This last goal, in particular, was totally unacceptable to Syria. First, the partition of Lebanon along religious lines might have a destabilizing effect on Syria's fragile sectarian edifice. Second, such an eventuality could undermine the concept of a Palestinian 'democratic secular state,' which formed the basis of Syria's vision of a Middle Eastern settlement. In Asad's words:

> Israel seeks to partition Lebanon in order to defeat the slogan of a democratic secular state – the slogan that we raise ... When Lebanon is partitioned, the Israelis will say: 'We do not believe these Arabs. If they could not coexist together, if the Muslim Arab could not coexist with the Christian Arab, how then can they coexist with the Jews and the non-Arab Jews who came from all spots of the earth, from the West and the East?' This slogan will then fall.[4]

Finally, the Syrians feared that the disintegration of Lebanon would provide Israel with an excuse to occupy southern Lebanon up to the Litani River, which in their view had been a long-coveted Zionist goal. Such an occupation would significantly increase Syria's strategic vulnerability by allowing Israel to 'bring the war into the rear of the Syrian-Lebanese Arab territories', while at the same time 'preventing the Syrian forces from using Lebanon in order to outflank the Israeli forces on the Golan'.[5] Syria's primary concern throughout the various stages of the civil war has therefore been to secure the continued existence of Lebanon as an independent Arab state. As the Syrian Foreign Minister, Abd Al-Khalim Khaddam, said: 'We will never allow the partition of Lebanon. Any move in this direction would mean our immediate intervention. Lebanon used to be a part of Syria and we will restore this fact, once the first attempt at partitioning takes place ... Either Lebanon remains united or it will have to return to Syria.'[6]

Until the autumn of 1975, either because of its preoccupation with the Egyptian drive for a separate deal with Israel, or as a result of the relative calm in Lebanon, Syria sought to keep its involvement in the Lebanese crisis to a minimum. Though sympathizing with the 'just cause of the Palestinian people' and rendering generous military support to the Palestinian organizations, the Syrians refrained from officially siding with the Muslim-leftist-Palestinian axis in its feud with the Christian-rightist camp, seeking instead to mediate a compromise between the belligerents. This policy clearly demonstrated the Syrian interest, which remained constant through the vicissitudes of the prolonged civil war: namely, to prevent either side from achieving a decisive victory which would undermine Lebanon's internal structure and invite an Israeli intervention.

The Syrian involvement in the Lebanese crisis acquired a new and deeper dimension in September 1975 with the signing of the Egyptian-Israeli agreement and the escalation of hostilities in Lebanon, both of which increased Syria's feeling of vulnerability and prompted it to move two Syrian-controlled Palestinian battalions – one belonging to the Palestinian Liberation Army (PLA) and the other to the Sa'iqa organization – into Lebanon in late September.[7] Though these forces were quickly withdrawn from Lebanon at the request of the Lebanese government, their introduction set an important precedent, to be repeated on a larger scale three months later: on 19 January 1976, following a widespread and successful Christian offensive, which the Syrians believed might lead to the *de facto* division of Lebanon, troops of the Yarmouq Brigade of the PLA again entered Lebanon to support the Muslim-leftist-Palestinian coalition. Helped by the arrival in Beirut of a Syrian delegation to mediate an agreement, the military intervention produced immediate results: the Christian offensive was checked, and on 22 January a ceasefire came into effect. A month later, on 14 February, the Lebanese President, Suleiman Faranjieh, announced a new 'national covenant', modelled on Syrian ideas and produced under Syrian auspices, which stipulated a more egalitarian sharing of power in Lebanon.

However, this 'national conciliation' proved short-lived. Frustrated by the limited nature of the reforms contained in the 'national covenant', the Muslim-leftist bloc sought to eradicate most of the political and economic benefits that remained in Christian hands. Consequently, in early March, the ceasefire broke down and, on 15 March, two days after two-thirds of the Lebanese Parliament had signed a petition calling for the resignation of President Faranjieh, leftist forces began a drive against the presidential palace at Baabda with the aim of overthrowing Faranjieh.

Paralleled by impressive Muslim military successes, which threatened to encircle the shrinking Christian enclave, this development triggered an immediate Syrian response. Again perceiving a danger of partition, this time emanating from the Muslim side, on 15 March Asad ordered the Sa'iqa and PLA units in Beirut to halt the leftist drive on Baabda. A few days later several regular Syrian commando battalions, disguised as PLA and Sa'iqa forces, entered Lebanon, and on 8 April a Syrian armoured brigade was moved to the Lebanese border and placed on an advanced state of alert (with some forty tanks reportedly deployed within Lebanese territory), in an attempt to deter the leftists from bringing down a newly attained truce.

Thus by late March 1976 Syrian policy towards the warring factions in Lebanon had been completely reversed, switching from close alignment with the Muslim-PLO coalition to support of the Christian camp. During the spring of 1976, the two former allies were steadily heading towards a collision, which eventually took place following the election on 8 May of Elias Sarkis, the Syrian-sponsored candidate, as president of Lebanon. Viewed by the leftists as a Syrian puppet, Sarkis's election led to an escalation of fighting which soon came to engulf the entire country. Following the failure of a mediation attempt by the Libyan Premier, Abd Al-Salam Jallud, and in the light of the inability of the Syrian and Syrian-controlled forces in Lebanon to contain the fighting, Damascus gradually reached the conclusion that the only way to stem the mounting tide of the Lebanese crisis was to launch a direct military intervention: on 1 June 1976 Syria's Third Armoured Division moved into Lebanon.

Syria's attempts to defuse the Lebanese crisis were viewed very favourably by Moscow. Sharing the Syrian view that the Lebanese civil war was the product of an 'imperialist-Zionist' plot, aimed at dividing the Arabs and diverting their attention 'from what is called partial solutions in the Middle East',[8] the Soviets had nothing against the accretion of influence by their major Middle Eastern ally in an essentially pro-Western country, especially since the Syrian policy appeared at the time to strengthen the Palestinian and leftist forces in Lebanon. Furthermore, they conceded that the 'strong geographical and historical ties' linking Syria and Lebanon, and the 'indivisibility' of the two countries' security, justified Syrian intervention in the face of Israel's secret intention to transform Lebanon into a 'springboard for aggression against Syria'.[9] Syria's keen interest in the Lebanese crisis was therefore not only fully justified, but was also in keeping with 'the principles of respect for sovereignty and independence'.[10]

In spite of its support for Syrian aims in Lebanon, Moscow grew uneasy about the course of the crisis in March 1976, when Syria turned against its former ally, the leftist-Palestinian coalition. True, this development had a positive facet: it diminished the likelihood of a Syrian-Israeli war, since Israel changed its position on Syrian military intervention in Lebanon from publicly proclaimed opposition to tacit approval. Israel was not interested in preventing Syrian action in favour of the Christians, provided that Syria recognized the 'red lines' concerning the 'rules of conduct', as well as the geographical boundaries within which Syrian operations would be tolerated.[11]

Yet the deepening rift between Syria and the 'progressive camp' – both major Soviet allies – put Moscow in a 'zero-sum' position, where support for one side would almost certainly alienate the other. Furthermore, this feud threatened to undermine the 'rejectionist front' which Moscow sought to cement, since Iraq, Libya and Algeria unequivocally sided with the leftist-Palestinian alliance. Finally, the Soviets were faced with a worrying convergence of Syrian and American interests, based on their joint goal of weakening the leftist-PLO forces.

In order to overcome these conflicting interests, the Soviets chose to support the Syrian line, while at the same time trying to avoid antagonizing their allies on the Left. Apart from underlining Syria's importance to the Soviet Union, which exceeded by far that of the PLO and the Lebanese Left put together, this policy reflected Soviet awareness of the reactive and reluctant nature of Syrian intervention in Lebanon. After all, it was the leftist camp, not Syria, which was responsible for the March 1976 escalation. Syrian military intervention, controversial as it was, was aimed at defusing a highly explosive situation and, in effect, constituted the only means that might save Lebanon from sliding into complete anarchy, if not from falling apart.

In keeping with this line, in mid-March the Soviets complimented Syria on persuading President Faranjieh to quit his post six months before the expiry of his term, describing this step as 'opening the way to resolving the crisis'.[12] Similarly, when the situation in Lebanon deteriorated, following the election of the Syrian-sponsored candidate, Elias Sarkis, to the presidency, the Soviets were quick to congratulate the new president on his election, describing this development as contributing to the de-escalation of tensions in the country.[13] Moreover, in an attempt to signal to the leftist-Palestinian bloc the desirability of collaborating with the newly elected president, *Pravda* claimed, on 13 May, that 'the progressive forces are ready to cooperate with the new administration'.

As late as 28 May 1976, three days before the Syrian Third Division began rolling into Lebanon, the Soviet media issued a strongly worded statement supporting Syrian pacification efforts in Lebanon and emphasizing Syria's leading role in the Arab world:

> The attempt to besmirch the Syrian mediation mission in Lebanon has been another aspect of imperialist and reaction pressure on Damascus. The enemies of the Arabs are using every means to stir up strife between the Lebanese and the Syrian nationalist forces with the aim of driving Damascus out of the anti-imperialist line, and destroying the [Palestinian] Resistance and the nationalist movement in Lebanon ... In their plots against Syria, imperialism and reaction are aiming in particular to undermine the Syrian National Progressive Front [whose unity] is the fundamental factor determining Syria's anti-imperialist course and ... enabling Syria to take the leadership of the liberation movement of all the Arab peoples.[14]

Against this backdrop one may question the common assumption that the direct Syrian intervention in Lebanon on 1 June 1976 took place in defiance of the Soviet position, with Moscow having no foreknowledge of it.[15] True, the Syrian entry into Lebanon started while the Soviet Premier, Aleksei Kosygin, was on his way from Baghdad to Damascus for a state visit. Yet this fact should be construed neither as an open rebuff to Kosygin nor as an intention to face him with a *fait accompli*. If anything, it reflected Syria's awareness of Moscow's delicate position. Since direct military intervention was perceived by Damascus as a means of last resort to prevent the disintegration of Lebanon, it *had* to be undertaken, and on the earliest date possible. The postponement of the Syrian intervention until Kosygin's departure would have portrayed this move as Soviet-Syrian collusion, thus putting the USSR in an awkward position *vis-à-vis* its Arab allies, on the one hand, and providing a pretext for increased Western (or Israeli) interference in the conflict, on the other. As things were, the USSR was able to keep its options open: to endorse the Syrian move at a later stage, or to distance itself from it – as indeed happened – should the need arise.

Moreover, the direct military intervention in Lebanon was not an isolated act; rather, it marked the culmination of a prolonged incremental intervention, which had hitherto received Soviet approval. Asad, therefore, had little reason to expect any Soviet opposition to his move, particularly in light of the unity of purpose achieved between the two countries regarding the Lebanese conflict.[16] Finally, the Syrian decision to intervene in Lebanon was preceded by intensive consultations with external actors. During the second half of May, Asad discussed the Lebanese developments with a whole host of Arab visitors, and even took care to clarify to the United States that any intervention in Lebanon 'was not aimed at Israel, but was meant to save Lebanon'.[17] Thus it is inconceivable that the Soviets were kept in the dark about the intervention: during May Asad held at least one meeting with the Soviet ambassador to Damascus.[18]

If the Syrian move into Lebanon created tension between the USSR and Syria, the two sides certainly failed to give it any public expression during Kosygin's visit to Damascus on 1–4 June. In an attempt to placate Kosygin, the Syrians agreed to include a statement in support of Geneva in the joint communiqué: a gesture they had evaded since late 1975. In return, Kosygin promised his country's continued assistance to 'friendly Syria in consolidating its defence potential'[19] and, perhaps most importantly, tacit support for the Syrian position in Lebanon. According to Syrian sources, Kosygin told Asad that while the USSR approved of Syrian actions in Lebanon, the Syrians should not expect any public declarations of support because of the Soviet commitment to the Palestinians.[20] Nevertheless the joint communiqué, issued at the close of Kosygin's visit, contained an overt, albeit veiled, endorsement of the Syrian action in Lebanon: 'The two sides expressed deep concern over the continuing crisis in Lebanon, which is a result of plotting by the forces of imperialism and Zionism. They confirmed their resolve to continue to work towards ending the bloodshed, restoring security and peace in Lebanon and ensuring its integrity, independence and sovereignty.'[21]

Soviet references to the Lebanese crisis following Kosygin's visit afford a further illustration of Moscow's support for Syria. According to the Soviet media, the Syrian intervention, which took place at the request of the 'official authorities' in Lebanon, was motivated by a 'national duty towards a sister nation', as well as 'compassion for the victims of the bloodshed between Arab brothers'. Aimed at 'normalizing the situation ... restoring order and facilitating the achievement of a ceasefire', this action took place only after 'all attempts by the national forces leading to a political settlement of the crisis have failed'. However limited in scope, the Syrian presence in Lebanon had exerted an immediate positive impact on the crisis by 'helping to ease the situation in a number of areas'. Hence, and given the Soviet 'thorough understanding' of the positions of those striving to 'achieve national unity' and to 'halt the bloodshed', Syria 'can always rely on the support of the USSR'.[22]

In addition, and in keeping with its policy in previous Middle Eastern crises (e.g. the 1970 Syrian invasion of Jordan, the October War), the USSR backed up its expressions of support with military activities. Between 28 May and 4 June 1976, the number of Soviet surface vessels in the Mediterranean was doubled and a naval presence was established opposite the Lebanese coast.[23] This augmentation, which came as a response to the growing Western, in particular American, naval presence in the eastern Mediterranean, aimed to signal to the Western powers the inadmissibility of any interference on their part in the Lebanese crisis. Its timing indicated a measure of Soviet foreknowledge, or at least anticipation, of the impending Syrian intervention. It is thus part of the overall pattern of support for the Syrian move.

In spite of this, Moscow was quick to distance itself from the operation when, within a few days, it got bogged down – with the invading forces suffering heavy casualties. In an official *Tass* statement published on 9 June, the Soviets, for the first time, expressed a direct, harsh criticism of the Syrian initiative:

> The Syrian Arab Republic has repeatedly stated that the mission of the troops sent by it to Lebanon was to help stop the bloodshed. Attention must, however, be drawn to the fact that an ever-swelling river of blood continues to flow in Lebanon today ... The first thing to be done in Lebanon, therefore, is to stop the bloodshed. All those parties involved in the Lebanese events, in one way or another, must cease fire forthwith.[24]

What were the reasons for this sudden change in the Soviets' policy? According to the Syrian Minister of Information, Ahmad Iskandar Ahmad, it 'could be traced back to their loss of naval facilities in

Alexandria and Marsa Matruh in Egypt. They needed bases in the Mediterranean. This was requested from Syria but was categorically refused. It seems, therefore, that the Russians hoped that in the eventuality of the Left and the Palestinians controlling Lebanon, they would be given naval facilities.'[25]

However intriguing, this view hardly seems plausible. First, if the desire for naval facilities did, in fact, lie at the root of the Soviets' behaviour, how can one explain their positive attitude towards Syria's Lebanese policy until 9 June, several months after Damascus had turned against the leftist-Palestinian coalition? Second, a leftist-Palestinian regime in Lebanon – a most remote eventuality, given both the Lebanese internal balance of forces and Israel's deep anxiety over events there – would not necessarily lead to Soviet access to naval facilities. Finally, the USSR had no need to place its hopes for naval facilities on the hypothetical policy of a non-established regime: in May 1976, Syria agreed to give the Soviet Mediterranean Squadron access to offshore facilities in the port of Tartus.

A more credible explanation for the Soviets' behaviour lies in their disappointment with the indecisive nature of the Syrian intervention. It should be remembered that their approval of Syria's incremental military interference in Lebanon had never been whole-hearted. Rather, it reflected the belief that, given the balance of forces, opportunities and risks, Syria's growing influence was the only factor that could prevent the disintegration of Lebanon. In supporting Syria's June 1976 intervention, they presumably anticipated that a limited, yet decisive, campaign would suffice to restore stability in Lebanon, without creating an irrevocable rift between Syria and the leftist camp or inciting external intervention. Once the Syrian operation got bogged down, they apparently concluded that Syria's policy in Lebanon had entered the stage of diminishing returns, and that its continuation could only worsen the situation. In other words, 'the Soviet Union was recoiling less from Syria's intervention in Lebanon than from its failure to be quick and bold enough to tip the scales and thereby spare Moscow an embarrassing situation.'[26]

Whatever the reasons for the Soviet change of tack, there is little doubt that the *Tass* statement of 9 June constituted a turning-point in Moscow's policy towards the Lebanese crisis. As early as 14 June, while avoiding a direct demand for a Syrian withdrawal, *Tass* cited

Ahmad Iskandar Ahmad as saying that the Syrian troops had entered Lebanon in order to create conditions 'for a dialogue among the Lebanese', and that once this aim had been attained the soldiers would leave immediately. The message of this reference was clear and unmistakable: since Syria had failed to produce the intended dialogue, there was no longer any justification for its military presence on Lebanese soil. Indeed, a month later, on 17 July, the Soviet news agency went a step further by arguing openly that a reconciliation between the Syrians and the PLO 'will become possible only after Syria pulls out all its forces from Lebanon'.

. By late August or early September 1976, the overt demand for a Syrian withdrawal had become a common motif in the Soviet media. 'No matter what considerations guided Damascus when it sent its troops into Lebanon,' wrote *Pravda* on 7 September, 'this decision proved to be harmful to the Palestinian movement, and enabled the right-wing forces to deal telling blows to the units of Palestinian and Lebanese national patriotic forces. It is clear why the Lebanese progressive organizations and the PLO, many Arab countries and other countries demand withdrawal of the Syrian units from Lebanon.' The extent of Soviet anxiety over Damascus's Lebanese policy was perhaps best illustrated by the hardening tone of the Soviet media, which began to put Syrian and Israeli behaviour towards the leftist-Palestinian alliance on a par. 'The Lebanese patriots and the Palestinians have just found themselves in a double encirclement,' argued Radio Moscow on 28 August, for while 'the Israeli ships blockade the southern coast of Lebanon to prevent the delivery of ammunition and food to the Lebanese national-patriotic forces and the Palestinian resistance units, retaliatory actions against the attacks of the Lebanese reactionaries are hampered by the Syrian control of strategic passes in the east, south and north of the country.'[27]

These public displays of dissatisfaction with the Syrian action in Lebanon were coupled with more tangible covert measures. According to Israeli sources, in mid-June 1976 the Soviets turned down a Syrian request for financial aid to offset the cost of their involvement in Lebanon.[28] During July, several missions were exchanged between Damascus and Moscow – without any visible results. Following some impressive Christian successes, gained through reliance on Syrian support, Foreign Minister Khaddam was summoned to Moscow, early in July, for discussions on the Lebanese situation.

The widening gap between the two sides was demonstrated by both the lack of any joint statement to summarize the talks and the criticism of Syria in the Soviet media throughout the visit. A return visit to Damascus later in the month by the Soviet Deputy Foreign Minister, Vasili Kuznetzov, proved equally unsuccessful.[29]

Soviet attempts at influence reached their climax on 11 July, when Brezhnev sent a personal letter to Asad in which he harshly criticized Syria's Lebanese policy, called for an immediate truce and implied Soviet sanctions would follow if Damascus did not withdraw its forces from Lebanon. 'We follow with concern Syria's position and orientations,' he wrote. 'We understand neither your line of conduct nor the aims which you are pursuing in Lebanon . . . If Syria persists in the course which it has taken, it will give the imperialists and their collaborators the opportunity to gain control over the Arab nations and progressive movements.' Therefore, he continued, 'we exhort the Syrian leaders to take all possible measures to end the military operations conducted against the resistance and the Lebanese national movement . . . You can contribute to this by *withdrawing your forces from Lebanon*. You have a good opportunity: the temporary presence of Arab forces in Lebanon.' 'It goes without saying,' he concluded, 'that we are *still* prepared to consolidate the links of friendship between our two countries . . . unless Syria behaves in such a way as to cause rifts in the relations between us.'[30] The seriousness of Brezhnev's threat became evident within a few days: from mid-July onwards, a significant slow-down in Soviet arms supplies to Syria, as well as hold-ups in the programme of technical assistance, was reported.[31]

This reprimand, unparalleled in scope and intensity during the Asad era, if not during the entire three decades of Soviet-Syrian relations, won Moscow precious little. Offended by what he perceived to be unjust criticism, Asad completely ignored the Soviet demand for withdrawal and intensified his drive towards a *Pax Syriana* in Lebanon. On 10 June the Syrian Progressive National Front responded to the *Tass* statement of the day before by issuing a pledge to continue Syria's policy in Lebanon.[32] Ten days later, during Asad's first visit to France – in itself a clear signal of Syria's determination to keep its political options open – the Syrian president had nothing but praise for the French mediation attempts in Lebanon. More annoying from the Soviet point of view, Asad managed to gain French tacit support for the 'Syrian efforts to help the warring parties in Lebanon to achieve a political solution to the Lebanese crisis that would preserve the unity and independence of Lebanon'. These efforts, Asad promised, would continue until Lebanon was 'rescued from its painful ordeal'.[33]

Given Moscow's deep concern over both Western interference in the Lebanese crisis and the continuation of the Syrian action, Asad's words constituted open defiance. Not only did he legitimize Western intervention in Lebanon, but he also aligned himself with a Western power on a policy totally rejected by the USSR.

Nevertheless, Asad was very careful to avoid an open rift with Moscow, refraining from overt criticism of the Soviet position, on the one hand, and making occasional gestures to the Soviets, on the other. Thus, for example, the joint statement issued on 1 July, at the close of a visit to Damascus by a Soviet Peace Committee delegation, contained Syrian support for the reconvening of the Geneva conference.[34] In mid-August, the Syrian media carried a harsh attack on America's Middle Eastern policy, accusing the United States of seeking to exploit the Lebanese events 'as a means to pressure the Arabs to accept capitulationist solutions'.[35] Two months later, in a policy statement published on 12 October, the Syrian government openly announced its interest in 'strengthening relations of cooperation with the friendly socialist states'.[36]

This combination of relentlessness and leniency, of determination and pragmatism, had a moderating impact on Soviet behaviour. The Syrian resilience clarified to Moscow the lengths to which it would have to go in order to twist Damascus's arm; Syria's avoidance of any brinkmanship in its relations with the USSR, however, demonstrated to Moscow the benefits of maintaining its special relationship with Damascus. This relationship seemed all the more important in the autumn of 1976 in the light of the Soviet intention to launch a fresh peace initiative for the Arab-Israeli conflict, which would need at least tacit Syrian approval.[37] Above all, the heavy blows dealt at the leftist-Palestinian camp from July to the end of September appeared to have driven the Soviets back to the conclusion that a *Pax Syriana* might, after all, be the least of all evils.

True, the early autumn of 1976 witnessed the continuation of Soviet public demands for a Syrian pull-back and, more important, the reiteration of this demand in yet another personal message from Brezhnev to Asad on 11 September.[38] Yet Soviet policy during that month showed a shift from exclusive pressures on Syria towards a more balanced position, aimed at mediating an arrangement between the warring factions in Lebanon.[39] In accordance with this line, in mid-September Farouq Kadoumi, head of the PLO's Political Department, was invited to Moscow, where he was apparently pressured by his Soviet hosts to moderate the PLO's position on a settlement with Syria.[40] The Soviet pressures on the PLO, reinforced by several meetings between Arafat and Vladimir Silkine, the Soviet *chargé d'affaires* in Beirut, seemed to bear fruit; on 24 September, the day after President Sarkis had entered office, Arafat sent a letter to the Lebanese president, informing him of the PLO's decision to adopt a unilateral ceasefire, as well as to conform to the agreements regulating Palestinian-Lebanese relations.

This development turned out to be very short-lived. On 28 September, the Syrian army, together with the Christians, launched a big offensive in the Lebanese mountains and managed to drive the leftist-Palestinian forces away from their strongholds controlling the Damascus-Beirut highway. The Syrian offensive, which took the Soviets by surprise, came at a very inopportune moment for Moscow. In the first place, the fresh deterioration in Lebanon diverted public attention from the Soviet peace initiative of 1 October, thereby playing an important role in its obstruction. Second, the offensive dealt a heavy blow to the evolving reconciliation between Syria and the leftist-Palestinian camp, subjected the Soviets to severe criticism by the PLO, and increased external interference, particularly Egyptian and Saudi, in the conflict.

Moscow's frustration over the Syrian move was quick in coming out. On 30 September, the same day that Syria stopped its offensive and called upon the Palestinians to enter into negotiations on a political settlement, the Soviet Afro-Asian Solidarity Committee issued a strongly worded statement on the Lebanese situation. Praising the PLO's announcement of a unilateral ceasefire as reflecting a 'high sense of responsibility', the statement blamed Damascus, along with the right-wing forces, for the escalation in Lebanon, accusing Syria of undermining the Arab struggle against Zionism and imperialism:

The fact that the Syrian troops which have been on Lebanese territory since last June are taking part in the present military operations against the Palestinian Resistance and the national patriotic forces of Lebanon is causing special concern to world

public opinion, a concern which is shared by the Soviet people.
It is absolutely clear that what is taking place in Lebanon today
is harming not only the Lebanese people, but the entire struggle
of the Arab peoples and states against Israeli aggression and for
a just political settlement in the Middle East.[41]

Repeated on several occasions in early October, the Soviet criticism[42] had no apparent impact on Asad. On the contrary, on 11
October he decided to launch yet another large military offensive,
which, within less than 48 hours, crushed the leftist-Palestinian
defences, leaving the Syrian forces at the outskirts of Beirut and
Sidon.

Though primarily motivated by the desire to improve Syria's
bargaining position in the all-Arab summit conference, scheduled to
open in Cairo on 18 October, the Syrian offensive was viewed by
Moscow as a rebuff to the Soviet position.[43] No less worrisome from
the Soviet standpoint was Asad's acceptance of a Saudi invitation to
attend the mini-summit in Riyadh on 16–18 October, with the
leaders of Egypt, Kuwait, Lebanon and the PLO. True, the conference saved the leftist-Palestinian alliance from total defeat, since
Asad, as a show of goodwill, ordered a general ceasefire until the
completion of the discussions in Riyadh. However, given its perception of Saudi Arabia as 'a sort of *chargé d'affaires* of the US
administration in the Middle East', the USSR resented the Saudi (as
well as Egyptian) interference in the Lebanese crisis, fearing that the
Riyadh conference would be exploited to tempt Syria into the
'reactionary camp'.[44]

In the event, once the Riyadh decisions were confirmed by the
Cairo summit conference a week later, the USSR had no choice but
to acquiesce: in October Moscow halted its overt criticism of Syria,
and from late 1976 onwards a gradual recognition of the legitimacy
of Syria's role in Lebanon emerged, with the Syrian troops being
referred to by the Soviet media as 'peacekeeping forces'. The arms
embargo, however, was not lifted until Asad threatened to cancel the
limited port services rendered to the Soviets in Tartus. Only then, in
early 1977, were arms shipments to Syria restored to their full extent
in accordance with previously signed agreements,[45] thereby removing a major obstacle from the path to Soviet-Syrian reconciliation.

4
TOWARDS A
BILATERAL TREATY

Reconciliation

The abating of the Lebanese crisis in late 1976 laid the basis for the recovery of Soviet-Syrian relations from the low point to which they had sunk following Syria's military intervention in Lebanon. With the Lebanese situation stabilized and the *Pax Syriana* recognized by the Arab world, the Soviets no longer had any reason to oppose the Syrian role. Moreover, given Syria's importance in the Middle East, Moscow could hardly afford to continue to alienate Damascus. The Soviets' sense of urgency in reaching a *rapprochement* with Syria was further enhanced by the election of Jimmy Carter to the presidency and the consequent thrust towards a peace settlement.

On the face of it, the inauguration of the Carter Administration in January 1977 was a positive development from the Soviet point of view. In contrast with the Nixon-Kissinger step-by-step diplomacy, Carter sought to achieve a comprehensive settlement through the Geneva framework; reacting against the Republican exclusionist approach, he viewed the USSR as a legitimate partner in his peace endeavour, as indicated by the (albeit short-lived) US-Soviet statement on the Middle East of 1 October 1977 (the Vance-Gromyko Statement), which set the boundaries of an Arab-Israeli settlement to be negotiated through the Geneva conference. Yet, knowing that without Syria – their dowry for a negotiated settlement – any political process would sooner or later be monopolized by the

United States, the Soviets sought to re-establish the close coordination and cooperation that had characterized Soviet-Syrian relations prior to the Lebanese crisis. Hence Moscow's tacit recognition of the Syrian presence in Lebanon from November 1976 onwards; hence, also, the lifting of the arms embargo and the invitation of Asad to Moscow in January 1977.

Moscow's shows of goodwill were not immediately reciprocated by Damascus. Having established control over Lebanon and set up a close pattern of cooperation with Jordan, Syria did not share the Soviet anxiety for a rapid reconciliation; instead it sought to 'forge an Arab bloc strong enough to become a regional power, able to stand up to pressure from either of the superpowers,'[1] by consolidating its relations with Saudi Arabia and reconstructing the strategic alliance with Egypt. On 18–21 December 1976, Asad paid an official visit to Cairo, where the two leaders decided to establish a Unified Political Command as a preliminary step on the road to Syrian-Egyptian unification. The harbinger of the renewed bilateral cooperation was the joint call for the reconvening of Geneva by March 1977, with the full participation of all parties, including the PLO.

Despite their long-standing advocacy of the need for both Arab solidarity and the reactivation of Geneva, the Soviets viewed with considerable concern the formation of the unified Arab front, which threatened to pull Syria into the Saudi-Egyptian-Jordanian camp. Especially alarming was the possibility that Syria, by way of adopting a unified approach with its Arab allies, would subordinate Palestinian interests to those of Jordan. Such apprehensions were not completely unfounded: not only did Syria, in early 1977, indicate a willingness to support the new American peace initiative, without coordinating its position with the USSR, but in January 1977 both Egypt and Syria spoke openly of a possible link between Jordan and a future Palestinian state. Moreover, Asad's insistence on a unified Arab delegation in Geneva – a reflection of his unequivocal rejection of any direct negotiations with Israel and his desire to prevent the Geneva conference from becoming a cover-up for separate deals with Israel – was interpreted by the Soviets as an indication of Syria's readiness to compromise the Palestinian cause. Indeed, contrary to numerous past pledges, in early 1977 Asad did not dismiss the possible reconvening of Geneva without the PLO. In his words:

If the PLO does not wish to take part in Geneva, we shall not exert any pressure to force it to participate. In that event the Arab states concerned will meet to decide what to do towards the liberation of the occupied Arab territories ... What should be clear is that the refusal of the PLO to participate will not cause any paralysis in the movement of the Arab states concerned.[2]

Dismayed as they were with the Syrian position, the Soviets avoided direct criticism of Asad, choosing instead to point their arrows at Egypt and other 'reactionary Arab circles'. Attributed solely to Anwar Sadat, the suggestion of a possible link between the Palestinian state and Jordan was denounced by the Soviet media as 'incompatible with the creation of a really independent Palestinian state'. Similarly, the idea of a joint Arab delegation to Geneva was ascribed not to Syria, but rather to 'reactionary circles' who sought to 'tame' the Palestinians.[3]

Luckily for Moscow, the 'Arab bloc' did not get very far. Asad's categorical insistence on a joint Arab delegation was totally unacceptable to Sadat, who resented the idea of constraining Egyptian diplomacy; this dispute injected a strong element of mutual distrust into Syrian-Egyptian relations, poisoning them from the outset. Saudi Arabia, on the other hand, was perceived by Asad as a hegemonic power, interested in 'calling the political tune in the area ... [by] attempting to play Syria off against Egypt and to keep both on a tight financial rein'.[4]

Syria was also quickly disillusioned with the USA's Middle Eastern policy. In March 1977, following Carter's public commitment to the concept of 'defensible borders' for Israel, Syria concluded that 'the difference between the policies of the US Democratic and Republican Parties is that the former has no clear features or specific identity, while both search for a solution at the expense of Arab rights and territories'.[5]

Subsequently, and without closing the door on the American peace efforts (after all, Jimmy Carter was the first American president to publicly recognize the need for a Palestinian homeland), Syria decided to improve its bargaining position *vis-à-vis* both superpowers by mending its fences with the USSR. In March 1977, two months after rejecting a Soviet request for a summit meeting,[6] Asad informed the USSR of his willingness to thaw bilateral relations, and on 18 April 1977 a high-ranking Syrian delegation, headed by Asad, arrived in Moscow for an official visit.

Despite the surfacing of differences between the two parties over a whole host of regional issues (e.g., turbulent Iraqi-Syrian relations), the wide coverage of the visit in the Soviet and Syrian media[7] and the text of the joint communiqué leave little doubt that a reconciliation had been achieved. In addition to securing Moscow's approval of the Syrian role in Lebanon, Asad managed to extract a Soviet pledge of economic, technical and military aid: on 21 April, the day before his departure, a bilateral agreement on technical and economic cooperation was signed; a new arms deal between the two countries was apparently also signed in late June 1977, during a visit to Moscow by the Syrian Defence Minister, Mustafa Tlas.[8] These gestures were repaid by vocal Syrian support for the earliest convocation of the Geneva conference and, more significantly, for the 'important role in preparing and holding the Geneva conference that the Soviet Union was called upon to play in its capacity as co-chairman'.[9]

Thus ended Asad's visit, leaving the two parties extremely pleased with its results. Emerging in the enviable position of being courted by both superpowers, Asad could proceed to reassert Syria's independence: on 9 May 1977 he met President Carter in Geneva for discussions which were described by the Syrian media as 'a decisive point in the development of the Middle East problem'.[10] The Soviets, for their part, could point out, with a real sense of satisfaction, that even such newspapers as the *Washington Post* and the *Christian Science Monitor*, which 'tried hard to misrepresent the real essence of Soviet-Syrian relations', were forced to acknowledge 'the coincidence of the views of Moscow and Damascus'.[11]

To be sure, Moscow would have preferred Syria to rely exclusively on its Soviet ally. But knowing how zealously Asad guarded Syrian independence (as illustrated by his defiance of the Soviet position during the 1976 Lebanese crisis), it had to be satisfied with the limited degree of coordination offered by Damascus.

On the other hand, being fully aware of Asad's uncompromising stance on both the framework of an Arab-Israeli settlement and the question of direct negotiations with Israel, the USSR had little reason to expect America to succeed where years of Soviet efforts had failed to produce results. Moreover, the election in May 1977 of

Menachem Begin, the leader of the right-wing Likud Party, as the Israeli premier was judged by the Soviets to be a serious constraint on the ability of the United States to produce an Arab-Israeli settlement.

This belief soon turned out to be well grounded. On 2 August 1977 Sadat met the American Secretary of State, Cyrus Vance, in Cairo and suggested – without prior consultation with Syria – that Arab and Israeli foreign ministers should meet in Washington in a 'working group' to discuss procedural matters before the reconvening of the Geneva conference. Quickly endorsed by Israel, the Egyptian suggestion was equally unacceptable to Moscow and Damascus. With the experience of the second disengagement talks still fresh in mind, both leaderships interpreted Sadat's move as an indication of Egypt's willingness to enter yet again into a separate, American-sponsored negotiations process, which might eventually culminate in a *Pax Americana.*

Upon arriving in Damascus, Secretary Vance was faced with an unequivocal Syrian rejection of the Egyptian idea. 'Undoubtedly, when Brother President Anwar Al-Sadat proposed the formation of this group, he wanted to give momentum to the peace process,' the Syrian leader told his American guest; however 'I do not know whether he assessed the negative aspects of this idea. From the first glance we, in Syria, do not see any great benefits to be derived from forming this group ... [therefore] no meetings will take place between the Arab foreign ministers and the foreign minister of Israel, either directly or indirectly.'[12]

The Syrian rejection, highly praised by Moscow, of the Egyptian initiative set in train a chain of events which was to overwhelm both Moscow and Damascus – indeed, the entire world. Confronted with Syrian intransigence, Carter, who remained committed to the attainment of a comprehensive settlement, proved reluctant to follow Kissinger's trail in pursuing a separate Egyptian-Israeli deal; instead he drew closer to the Soviet Union in an attempt to reach a superpower consensus on both the components of a political settlement and the road to its attainment. This resulted in the Vance-Gromyko Statement. The Egyptian reaction to the American policy was abrupt: on 9 November 1977, having failed to convince Syria (and Israel) to hold preliminary talks on the agenda of the Geneva conference, and viewing the Vance-Gromyko Statement as a conspiracy by the superpowers to impose a settlement, Sadat announced his willingness to go to Jerusalem and talk to the parliament there, if it would help the cause of peace. Ten days later, having received an official invitation from Premier Begin, Sadat arrived in Jerusalem.

November 1977 and after

Sadat's visit to Jerusalem introduced a profound, though not precipitous, change in the balance of Soviet-Syrian relations, which was to have lasting effect. Until November 1977 the USSR's dependence on Syria – the only remaining pro-Soviet country involved in the Arab-Israeli conflict – exceeded by far Syria's anxiety to maintain close relations with Moscow. This imbalance was reversed following Sadat's visit to Jerusalem, as Syria's growing sense of vulnerability narrowed the gap between Soviet and Syrian assessments of the value of their bilateral relationship.

For Syria, the visit was most traumatic. Apart from breaking the most sacred Arab political and ideological taboo, Sadat's move undermined Syria's ability to advance its own national goals. Differences, distrust and hostility apart, Asad never forgot that it had been the alliance with Egypt that had made Syria's greatest achievement – the October War – possible. Egypt's crucial role in Syria's 'grand strategy' was clearly evident from Asad's willingness, if not eagerness, to rebuild the strategic alliance with Egypt in late 1976, in spite of the signing of the second Egyptian-Israeli disengagement agreement in September 1975.

Now that Sadat had broken the 'rules of the game', Asad was forced to conclude that the strategic balance between the Arabs and Israel had been seriously upset and that Syria *alone* would have to shoulder the burden of confronting Israel.[13] And since the attainment of this goal required an unprecedented expansion of Syria's military power, Damascus's dependence on Soviet military aid grew considerably, thus enhancing Moscow's bargaining position *vis-à-vis* Syria.

While joining Syria in opposing Sadat's peace initiative,[14] the Soviets did not share the intensity of Asad's anxiety over the adverse implications of the visit. On the contrary, the opportunities offered by Sadat's visit appeared to Moscow to exceed its potential risks. In the first place, well aware of Begin's 'hawkish' views, the Soviets probably assessed that the Israeli-Egyptian dialogue was doomed to fail. Second, given America's initial coolness towards Sadat's initiative (on 22 November 1977 the US Deputy Secretary of State,

Warren Christopher, voiced strong support for the Vance-Gromyko Statement and for the Soviet role in a Middle East peace settlement), the USSR presumably judged the establishment of a *Pax Americana* to be unlikely; indeed, the Soviets remained optimistic until quite a late stage that the Carter Administration would do its best to bring the Egyptian-Israeli dialogue back into the Geneva framework. Finally, and most importantly, Sadat's visit gave the USSR a unique opportunity to rally its Arab supporters into a cohesive front, in an attempt to undermine the evolving peace process. The months following the visit witnessed a pilgrimage of delegations from Syria, Iraq, Libya, Algeria, South Yemen and the PLO to Moscow, where they were promised political and material support. The USSR voiced warm praise for the Tripoli and the Algiers summits, 2–5 December 1977 and 2–5 February 1978, which established the Front for Steadfastness and Confrontation and laid down the principles for its operation.[15]

Moscow's decision to align itself with the rejectionist front must have been an easy one. Support for the Egyptian initiative would have endangered Moscow's position amongst its Arab allies, while it was unlikely to have produced any rewards from Sadat, given the state of Soviet-Egyptian relations at the time. Moreover, the Soviets apparently reasoned that once the Egyptian-Israeli dialogue had run its unsuccessful course, the USSR would be in a better position to push for the revival of the Geneva process. Even if – the worst scenario – the Egyptian-Israeli negotiations were to culminate in a separate deal under American auspices, this would not necessarily contradict Soviet Middle Eastern interests. Assuming that Egypt's example would not be followed by other Arab states (as indeed happened), a separate Egyptian-Israeli agreement could only be expected to add fuel to Arab rejectionism. This, in turn, would increase Egypt's isolation, alienate more Arab countries from the United States, including perhaps some conservative regimes, and present the USSR as the champion of the Arab cause.

In these circumstances, a balance was struck between the USSR's reliance on Syrian political support and Syria's growing dependence on Soviet military backing. On the one hand, Syria retained its pivotal role in Soviet Middle Eastern strategy. Being the only member of the Front for Steadfastness and Confrontation immediately adjoining Israeli territory, Syria's opposition to, or alternatively support for, the Egyptian-Israeli peace process could influence more than anything else the success or failure of the anti-Sadat campaign. Further, as the sole member of the Front recognizing, however reluctantly, Resolution 242 and supporting the Geneva conference, Syria might be a crucial ally in any future Soviet thrust towards a comprehensive peace settlement.

On the other hand, Moscow's awareness of Syria's growing need for military support enabled it to charge higher prices for its services to Damascus. If the attainment of strategic parity with Israel had become Syria's primary foreign policy goal, and if the USSR was the only country capable of making this goal feasible, then the Soviets had to be more richly rewarded, on the bilateral level as well as the regional. Reinforced from 1978 to 1980 by the growing domestic and regional difficulties facing the Asad regime, this reasoning manifested itself in an increasing number of Syrian allusions to the possibility of raising Soviet-Syrian relations to a higher, perhaps even formalized, level.

Towards a Friendship and Cooperation Treaty
The USSR's interest in formalizing relations with Damascus through the conclusion of a Friendship and Cooperation Treaty can be traced back to the early 1970s. In May 1972, a year after the conclusion of a bilateral treaty with Egypt and a month after the signing of a Soviet-Iraqi treaty, Moscow reportedly approached Damascus with a request for it to sign a Friendship and Cooperation Treaty.[16] The firm, but polite, Syrian refusal did not dissuade the Soviets from raising the issue two months later, during Asad's visit to Moscow, only to be turned down again. 'Syria and the USSR are friends,' Asad told the Soviets, 'and a real friendship does not require any treaties. The joint experiences and intensive interaction are as meaningful as a treaty, and there is no need to formalize them by signed documents.'[17] Practical considerations apart (e.g., curtailment of the flow of funds from the conservative Arab oil countries), Asad was most anxious not to compromise Syria's sovereignty in a manner that could tarnish its position or its image in the Arab world.

Thus Asad was no more forthcoming to Soviet approaches in the years after 1973 than he had been before the war. Even the signing of the second Egyptian-Israeli disengagement agreement, in September 1975, did not make him change his mind: in October 1975 Asad rejected another request for a bilateral treaty.[18] Towards the end of the decade, however, the Syrian position was reversed. Alarmed by the upset of the regional balance of power following Egypt's 'defection from the Arab camp', on the one hand, and by mounting violent opposition to his regime, on the other, Asad began to view a bilateral treaty with the USSR as an asset rather than a liability.

With Syrian forces bogged down in Lebanon in a futile strife against the Christian Maronite militias, backed by Israel; with Iraq distinctly hostile, Jordan supporting the Muslim Brotherhood in its struggle against the Syrian regime, and relations with the PLO in a state of turmoil, Syria's sense of vulnerability rose sharply. Together with the spectre of the Israeli threat, which at the time loomed greater than ever before, and the inherent weakness and growing fragmentation of the Front for Steadfastness and Confrontation, these factors explain Asad's anxiety to seek refuge in a closer relationship with the USSR. In these circumstances, the possible infringement on Syria's sovereignty of a bilateral treaty was dismissed out of hand, on the grounds that in those trying days of a growing Israeli threat to the Arab world, it was imperative for all progressive forces to draw a clear distinction between friend and foe, rather than to dwell on formalistic niceties. In Asad's words: 'By saying that we are nonaligned, we are not equating the two superpowers. It is impossible and inconceivable to equate the one who gives arms to our enemy to occupy our territories with the one who gives us arms and political support ... Syria befriends those who befriend it and is hostile to those who are hostile to it.'[19]

Indeed, from late 1978 onwards it became increasingly evident that Syria was not merely after a standard Friendship and Cooperation Treaty, but rather sought to tie the USSR to a more binding pact, particularly concerning defence. On 7 September 1978, following reports that America intended to sign a defence pact with Israel in order to allay the latter's apprehensions over its national security and thus to strengthen its willingness to make territorial concessions, Abd Al-Khalim Khaddam, the Syrian Foreign Minister, called upon the members of the Front for Steadfastness and Confrontation to respond in kind by entering into defence agreements with the USSR.[20] A month later, during a summit meeting in Baghdad of the Front's foreign ministers, Khaddam reportedly threatened that Syria would join the Warsaw Pact, should it fail to receive the necessary support from its Arab allies.[21]

Taking their cue from these statements, the Soviets apparently took up the issue of a Friendship and Cooperation Treaty during Asad's visit to Moscow on 5–6 October 1978,[22] only to realize that the Syrian leader was not yet ready to take the crucial decision. It required another crisis in Soviet-Syrian relations – in late November 1978 the Syrian Chief of Staff, General Hikmat Shihabi, arrived in Moscow to work out the details of a new large-scale arms deal, but was reportedly turned down by the Soviets, thereby sparking off an angry Syrian response[23] – and the culmination of the Egyptian-Israeli negotiations in a formal peace treaty in March 1979 to drive the Syrians and the Soviets closer together. On 24 March 1979, a day after the conclusion of the Egyptian-Israeli peace treaty, Andrei Gromyko arrived in Damascus for an unexpected visit. Though it avoided any commitments to Syria in the military sphere, the official statement on the talks indicated a joint determination to accelerate the intensification of bilateral relations.[24]

Gromyko's visit was followed by indications of Soviet readiness to enhance Syria's military potential. During the first half of 1979, for example, the Soviet media carried a number of references to the detrimental impact on the regional strategic balance of Egypt's 'betrayal' of the Arab cause. By deserting the Arab camp, it was argued, Egypt exposed Syria to Israeli 'tactics of intimidation', aimed at forcing Syria to give up its 'principled stand'. In these circumstances, it would be unrealistic to expect the USSR to remain an 'indifferent spectator' of Middle Eastern events.[25] The seriousness of this assertion was demonstrated in August 1979 by the arrival in Syria of the first consignment of T-72 tanks – the most advanced Soviet-made model.[26]

But the real breakthrough in Soviet-Syrian procurement relations was accomplished in October 1979 during another visit by Asad to Moscow. Scheduled to take place in late June and postponed as a result of the turbulence in Syria, the visit bore abundant fruit: apart from writing off $500 million of Syria's military and economic debts, and signing generous economic and technological agreements,[27] the two parties concluded their largest arms deal until then, thus opening a new qualitative stage in Syria's military build-up. As a result of the treaty, the Syrian armed forces absorbed approximately 1,400 tanks (including 800 T-72s), 200 combat aircraft (including MiG-25 and SU-20/22), 2,000 armoured vehicles and 1,700 artillery pieces.[28]

Just as the October 1979 visit constituted an important landmark in the evolution of Soviet military support for Syria, so it also marked a watershed in Soviet and Syrian approaches towards the issue of a bilateral treaty. If until that visit it had been the USSR that had been the driving force behind the quest for a bilateral treaty, from that time onwards it was Syria that worked to bring it about. Thus it is not inconceivable that Brezhnev's evasion of Asad in October 1979, explained by the Soviets on grounds of poor health, emanated from his reluctance to give a flat refusal to Syrian requests for a bilateral treaty.

Moscow's decreasing interest in a Friendship and Cooperation Treaty was understandable. However important, a bilateral treaty with Syria had never been perceived by the Soviets as a top priority foreign policy goal. Until October 1973, while the USSR was preoccupied with the prevention of a new Arab-Israeli conflagration, Syria was not viewed as important enough to justify a large Soviet campaign to push it into a bilateral treaty. Conversely, given Syria's ascendancy in Soviet Middle Eastern interests in the aftermath of the October War, the USSR was careful not to antagonize its major regional ally by pushing the issue of the treaty too hard. Furthermore, Soviet-Syrian relations during the Asad era never reached such a low ebb as to create a desperate Soviet need for a formal treaty, as had happened with Egypt. Consequently, differences over the conclusion of such a treaty fell short of developing into a real irritant between Moscow and Damascus, with the USSR foregoing employment of the 'stick', and limiting its attempts at persuasion to the use of the 'carrot'.

The significant weakening of Asad's domestic and regional position in the late 1970s served as a further restraint to the Soviet drive towards a bilateral treaty. A treaty with a confident and strong Syria, which was playing a leading role in the Arab world, was one thing, but an accord with an isolated leader, who faced an imminent threat of dethronement, was quite another. Moreover, familiar with Asad's propensity for independent conduct, the Soviets apparently feared that a precipitous reaction on his part to the threats facing the regime might drag them into an undesirable predicament. Therefore, from late 1979 onwards the Soviet Union surrenderd the initiative in the quest for a treaty to Syria, and adopted an essentially reactive position on the issue.

This change of roles between the Soviet Union and Syria is clearly demonstrated by the tone and scope of coverage given to the issue of a bilateral treaty in Moscow and Damascus during the months preceding its conclusion. While Syrian officials and the state-controlled Syrian media referred openly and widely to the forthcoming treaty, the Soviet media, as well as government figures and officials, ignored the subject completely. The Soviet media praised the measures taken by the Syrian regime against the Islamic Brotherhood, condemning this organization as an American proxy; they supported Syria's defiance of America's Middle Eastern policy and hailed the Syrian friendship with the USSR. Yet they never mentioned the intensive discussions on a Friendship and Cooperation Treaty that were under way at the time, nor did they give any indication of Soviet support for such an eventuality.[29]

In order to convince the USSR of the desirability of a bilateral treaty, Syria identified itself increasingly with the Soviet cause from late 1979 onwards. Thus, for example, not only did Syria abstain, alongside the other members of the Front for Steadfastness and Confrontation, from joining the overwhelming majority of the UN General Assembly in denouncing the Soviet invasion of Afghanistan,[30] but Syrian diplomats at the UN were reported to have lobbied on behalf of the USSR prior to the vote.[31] Moreover, Syria quickly established itself as the leader of the camp supporting the Soviet action. On 16 January, two days after the UN condemnation of the Soviet invasion, the foreign ministers of the Front convened in Damascus, where they issued a joint statement denouncing criticism of the USSR as an 'uproar fabricated by world imperialism', and called upon the Islamic Conference Organization (ICO) to postpone its emergency session, scheduled for 26 January, 'to a later date', as well as to move the projected venue from Islamabad, Pakistan, to Saudi Arabia. The foreign ministers also suggested widening the ICO agenda beyond the Afghanistan question to include the issue of the Arab-Israeli conflict, on the one hand, and American military threats to the Middle East, on the other.

Despite the ICO's willingness to widen the agenda of the forthcoming conference to include the issues of Palestine and Jerusalem, as well as to postpone the opening of the sessions by one day, Syria – unlike Algeria, Libya and the PLO – decided not to send delegates to Islamabad. Furthermore, by way of demonstrating its resentment of the anti-Soviet campaign, Syria invited the Soviet foreign minister to Damascus on 27–29 January, to coincide with the Islamic Conference. Thus, when the Conference came out with a call for the immediate and unconditional withdrawal of all Soviet troops from Afghanistan, Syria and the USSR issued a joint communiqué condemning 'the continuing campaign of the imperialist forces, headed by the United States, which are exhibiting false concern for Islam, while at the same time supporting the seizure by Israel of Islamic temples in Jerusalem'.[32]

Syria's unequivocal support for the Soviet invasion of Afghanistan was not an isolated episode; rather it reflected a steady drive towards a closer alliance with Moscow which was to gain momentum in the following months. In a policy statement, issued on 18 February 1980, the Syrian government declared its intention to 'continue to strengthen the ties of friendship and cooperation with the socialist-bloc countries, headed by the USSR'.[33] A month later, the Syrian Premier, Abd Al-Rauf Kasim, openly alluded to the possibility of signing a bilateral treaty with the USSR, 'should the United States escalate its aggression' against Syria.[34] If there remained any doubts regarding Syria's willingness to conclude a Friendship and Cooperation Treaty with the Soviet Union, they were completely dispelled by Asad, who, in a public speech on 23 April, revealed that a decision on raising Soviet-Syrian relations to a 'higher and advanced level' had already been taken, in accordance with 'the interest of our nation and in fulfillment of our aspirations, cause and morals'.[35]

Indeed, the implementation of Syria's decision to upgrade its relations with the USSR to a 'higher qualitative level' was quick and determined: amidst a growing number of references, by both leading government officials and the state-controlled media, to the consolidation of Soviet-Syrian relations,[36] some ten visits were exchanged between Damascus and Moscow from April to October 1980.[37] In mid-May Khaddam hinted that discussions on upgrading bilateral relations were already under way, and in August the 13th National Congress of the Ba'th Party gave formal sanction to the intention to develop further Soviet-Syrian ties.[38]

Concluded on 8 October 1980, the Soviet-Syrian Treaty of Friendship and Cooperation constituted an uneasy compromise, the outcome of a balance of mutual weakness. Reluctant as it was to sign a treaty at that time, the USSR could not afford to turn down its major Middle Eastern ally. Syria, for its part, unable to harness an unequivocal Soviet commitment to its national security, in the form of a defence pact, had to content itself with a 'standard' Third World Friendship and Cooperation Treaty.

5

FROM CRISIS TO WAR

In the two years from the signing of the Friendship and Cooperation Treaty to the death of the ailing Brezhnev in November 1982, the newly attained agreement – in fact, the entire delicate web of Soviet-Syrian relations – was subjected to repeated tests. Tensions, crises and ultimately war made it imperative for Moscow to tread cautiously between the need to harness the treaty for Syria's security and the need to avoid being drawn into too great a commitment.

Indeed, it was not long before this dilemma was to give rise to conflicting interpretations of Soviet military and strategic obligations towards Syria. Whereas the Syrians depicted the treaty as embodying a far-reaching Soviet undertaking to redress the strategic imbalance caused by Egypt's desertion of the Arab camp, by ensuring that 'any aggression to which Syria will be exposed will not be faced by Syria separately,'[1] the Soviets sought to downplay the extent of their commitment by highlighting the international, rather than the bilateral, ramifications of the treaty.[2] Whilst Syria viewed the provision for consultation and cooperation as a means to harness Soviet support for its foreign policy ventures, the Soviet Union regarded this stipulation as a useful mechanism for crisis management.

As early as October 1980, during Asad's visit to Moscow, Brezhnev hinted that dramatic changes in the nature of Soviet wartime commitment to Syria should not be expected to follow from the bilateral treaty. 'The task of the Soviet-Syrian treaty', he said, 'is to help improve the situation in the Near East and establish there a real and just peace. This treaty has no other objectives and it is not directed against third countries. *This is a treaty in the name of peace, not in the name of war.*[3] Similarly, the Soviet media vehemently denied reports in the Western and Arab press about the existence of secret clauses in the bilateral treaty, allegedly establishing new and higher limits for Soviet wartime support for Syria.[4]

That the Friendship and Cooperation Treaty implied neither automatic and unconditional Soviet support for every Syrian move, nor a more binding commitment to Syria's security beyond the already established pattern, became evident from Moscow's behaviour in a series of crises which embroiled Syria during the late Brezhnev years. Having no role in the initiation of any of these conflicts, the Soviets chose to adhere to their own interpretation of the treaty, using it as a restraint rather than as a catalyst, as both an umbrella for coordination and a channel through which to influence Syria. The first clear sign of Moscow's restrictive interpretation of the bilateral treaty came within two months of its conclusion, when the Soviets refrained from siding with Syria in its open feud with Jordan.

The Syrian-Jordanian crisis
On 25 November 1980, allegedly in response to Jordan's continued aid to the Muslim Brotherhood (which organized resistance to the Asad regime), and following a steady deterioration in Syrian-Jordanian relations, Syrian armoured units were deployed along the common border with Jordan, thus bringing relations between the two countries to their lowest ebb since September 1970.

The Syrian move was viewed by Moscow with much concern. Coming in the wake of the Iraqi invasion of Iran (in September 1980), the Syrian-Jordanian escalation threatened to create another focus of tension in the Middle East, thereby diverting Arab attention from the separate Egyptian-Israeli peace treaty and, in consequence, eroding the unity of the fragile anti-Sadat coalition. In addition, Syria's pressures on Jordan checked the steady warming of Soviet-Jordanian relations, bringing the United States and Jordan together again after a period of chill following the Camp David accords. Thus, in response to the Syrian action, King Hussein postponed his long-awaited trip to Moscow (which eventually took place in May 1981), while at the same time approaching Washington for military support. Although this development was not necessarily negative for Syria, which must have regarded the worsening of Soviet-Jordanian relations as improving its own bargaining position, the Soviets were obviously dissatisfied with this possible narrowing of their regional options. Last, and perhaps most important, was Moscow's fear that the crisis would lead to open hostilities, resulting in an Israeli intervention and the need for Soviet interference in yet another Middle Eastern war.

Given these considerations, the USSR did its best to contain the crisis. Not only did it forgo any public endorsement of the Syrian position, but the low-key coverage of the crisis in the Soviet media reflected its strictly neutral stand towards the rival parties.[5] Aimed at signalling the intensity of Moscow's displeasure with the deterioration of Syrian-Jordanian relations, this public neutrality was paralleled by the arrival in Damascus on 2 December of the Soviet First Vice-President and Alternate Member of the Politburo, Vasily Kuznetsov. To judge by the overall tone of Kuznetsov's public pronouncements, which laid a heavy emphasis on both the need for a peaceful settlement of inter-Arab problems and the peaceful aims of the bilateral treaty,[6] there is little doubt that the Soviet official requested his Syrian hosts to exert the utmost restraint.

Although it is by no means clear whether Asad entertained any intentions of attacking Jordan, the fact that Syria's move was met by chill on the part of its main international ally, and furthermore that Moscow exploited the new treaty as a means to constrain Syrian policy, appears to have severely limited Damascus's manoeuvrability. By emphasizing the peaceful nature of the treaty at the peak of the crisis, the USSR prevented Syria from sheltering behind the treaty, thereby considerably weakening Damascus's bargaining position *vis-à-vis* Jordan. Indeed, during the entire period of tension (25 November – 10 December) Syria refrained from any public mention of the bilateral treaty. As things turned out, this highly circumspect Soviet behaviour remained a rather isolated episode in Soviet-Syrian relations – as the 'missile crisis' of May 1981 made clear. On that occasion, while still anxious to downplay the treaty and to employ it as a coordination mechanism for crisis containment, the USSR did not fail to indicate, in the most unequivocal way, where its sympathies lay.

The Soviets and the missile crisis

On 28 April 1981, in response to ostensibly desperate pleas for support by the Christian Phalanges militia, Israel attempted to pressure Damascus to loosen its siege of the Christian town of Zahla in the Beq'a valley by downing two Syrian transport helicopters, which were on a supply mission in nearby Mount Sanin. Syria reacted within less than 24 hours by moving mobile SA-6 surface-to-air missile batteries into Lebanon and deploying them near Zahla, in positions prepared a few weeks earlier.[7] Viewing this as a gross violation of the unwritten Syrian-Israeli rules of the game in Lebanon, which could severely constrain Israel's aerial activity over that country, Premier Menachem Begin instructed the Israeli air force on 30 April to destroy the newly deployed missiles. When this plan was held up by bad weather conditions, the issue developed into an open confrontation, with Begin pledging to destroy the missiles unless they were removed from Lebanon, and Asad adamantly rejecting this demand. The public squabbling was accompanied by a series of military actions which brought the two countries closer to war than at any time since 1974. These included partial mobilization of reserve forces by both sides, deployment of additional Syrian surface-to-air missiles in Lebanon and along the Syrian-Lebanese border, reinforcement of the Syrian forces in the Beq'a and, finally, employment of anti-aircraft fire against Israeli planes flying over Lebanon.

Although it endangered the delicate Syrian-Israeli *modus vivendi* in Lebanon, the gathering storm over this country posed less of a problem to the Soviet Union than the Syrian-Jordanian border tension of November 1980. At least this time Moscow was spared the dilemma of having to choose between two Arab protagonists. Moreover, as the US became increasingly identified with its Israeli ally during the crisis, the USSR had good reason to anticipate an improvement in its regional standing, provided, of course, that events did not get out of control. Thus the Soviets chose not to cooperate with their rival superpower, but rather to try to defuse the conflict on their own through the coordination mechanism offered by the Soviet-Syrian treaty. This, in turn, meant that difficult choices had to be made between several conflicting factors: between the obligation to back Syria's position and the urgent need to contain the crisis; between the desire to frustrate US mediation efforts and the wish to benefit from them, at least through the restraining of Israel.

From the very outset of the missile crisis, the USSR sought to discredit America's suitability to play the role of impartial mediator between Israel and Syria. 'It is highly significant that the US leaders are by no means preparing to make the high-handed Israeli aggressors see reason,' argued *Tass* on 5 May, as the special American envoy to the Middle East, Philip Habib, was preparing to leave for the region; 'they openly support Tel Aviv's ultimatum, but before giving the "green light" to Israel to carry out a strike on Lebanon, they would like "to have more time" for "diplomatic efforts", with the help of which it is intended to force the Lebanese side to accept Tel Aviv's conditions and to impose on the Lebanese people US-Israeli diktat.'

The American attempt to twist Syria's arm, the Soviets believed, was all the more deplorable given that the removal of the Syrian missiles would mean the 'virtual disarmament of the national patriotic forces and the joint Arab peacekeeping forces in Lebanon'; and since the Arab deterrent force had been introduced into Lebanon at the request of the lawful Lebanese government, to ensure peace and security, its weakening would necessarily destabilize the situation there. Syria's firm stand in the face of the Israeli and American threats could not, therefore, be considered a catalyst to war. On the contrary, it is a 'purely defensive measure . . . [which] falls short of threatening Israel's security in any way' and which aims at 'securing [Syrian] lands occupied in 1967, and establishing a just peace in the Middle East'. In other words, by adhering to its position in Lebanon, Syria was not merely pursuing its own national interest, but rather acting as the 'main bulwark' of the progressive Arab camp, thereby deserving the maximum support of the Arab countries.[8]

This verbal support was accompanied by a series of political, military and even economic moves, designed to demonstrate the extent of Soviet backing for Syria. On 6 May, the Soviet First Deputy Foreign Minister, Georgii Kornienko, arrived in Damascus for a three-day visit, presented by the two parties as coming within the framework of the Friendship and Cooperation Treaty.[9] The exchange of several high-ranking political and military delegations accounts for the close coordination of Soviet-Syrian positions during the crisis; these included the visits of the Soviet Chief of Staff, Nikolai Ogargov, and the Syrian Minister of Defence, Mustafa Tlas, to Damascus and Moscow respectively, and, according to some sources, a 24-hour trip by Asad himself to Moscow.[10]

In addition, and by way of counterbalancing the American naval presence in the eastern Mediterranean, the Soviets augmented their Mediterranean squadron to its highest level in four years and deployed a naval task force – reportedly including the helicopter carrier, *Moskva* – off the Lebanese coast.[11] Another demonstration of support, albeit of an indirect nature, was the signing on 14 May of a Soviet-Syrian agreement on economic and technical cooperation, as well as the two countries' pronounced intention to boost bilateral trade by 150 per cent in 1981–5.[12]

Last but not least, the USSR rapidly increased its military support for Syria in early July, when the essentially abated crisis appeared to be rekindling, following renewed threats by the re-elected Menachem Begin to destroy the Syrian missiles. The new Soviet measures included the acceleration of arms supplies by a special airlift and, more significant, the staging of a joint Soviet-Syrian amphibious exercise on 6–7 July.[13]

Thèse strong demonstrations of support notwithstanding, the USSR did not fail to indicate to all parties involved its clear interest in containing the crisis. During Kornienko's visit to Damascus, the Syrians were informed of Moscow's reluctance to see the crisis escalating into an open conflagration,[14] and this position found a clear echo in Soviet statements which, while voicing strong support for Syria and condemning the United States and Israel, warned against the danger of the situation worsening, and advocated a peaceful resolution to the conflict.[15] On 22 May, the missile crisis was referred to by Leonid Brezhnev in person. Speaking at Tbilisi, on the 60th anniversary of Soviet power in Georgia, the Soviet leader displayed deep anxiety over the Lebanese tragedy, which, in his words, was taking place in close proximity to the USSR's southern borders. 'One rash move', he warned, 'and the flames of war could envelop the entire Near East, and one cannot know how far the sparks of the fire could fly.'[16]

The only way to eliminate this threat to international peace, in Brezhnev's view, was to convene an international conference on the Middle East, along the principles outlined at the 26th CPSU congress three months earlier. The fact that neither of Brezhnev's references to the crisis contained any allusion to the Soviet-Syrian bilateral treaty served to illustrate an important aspect of Moscow's behaviour: namely, the attempt to play down Soviet military engagement in the crisis, as well as to underline the irrelevance of the Friendship and Cooperation Treaty to the situation in Lebanon. Thus, while occasionally implying recognition of the unique strategic significance of the Beq'a for Syrian security,[17] the Soviet media repudiated as 'an obvious lie' Israeli radio reports that referred to the Soviet Ambassador to Lebanon, Alexander Soldatov, as having stated that any military intervention in the Beq'a would prompt the USSR to study the question of increasing military aid to Syria.[18] Similarly, Damascus's claim that 'Syria has succeeded in mobilizing all the positive elements, particularly the treaty of friendship and cooperation with the USSR, in support of its decisions and political and military moves'[19] was preceded by a Soviet assertion that 'the recent developments [in Lebanon] are unrelated to the Soviet-Syrian treaty.'[20] Moscow also vehemently – and justifiably – rejected Begin's allegations about the presence of Soviet advisers among the Syrian forces in Lebanon.[21]

Soviet defensiveness was directed not only at Damascus, but also at Jerusalem, which, the Soviets believed, held the key to the escalation or de-escalation of the crisis. Although it lacked both direct influence over Israel's policy and insight into the Israeli decision-making process (diplomatic relations had been severed in 1967), the USSR was anxious to prevent a sudden action against Syria; it therefore took care to alleviate fears in Jerusalem of a Soviet-backed Syrian move. Hence the relative restraint of Soviet attacks on Israel compared with those on the United States; hence Brezhnev's unexpected announcement, at the height of the crisis, of the USSR's interest in improving relations with Israel. 'We . . . want good relations with all countries in the . . . Middle East,' he stated at a dinner on 26 May in honour of King Hussein; 'this concerns those with whom we have friendship and mutual understanding and those with whom relations have not been developed or are so far non-existent. This also concerns Israel, if, naturally, it abandons the policy of seizing other peoples' lands and follows a peaceful, rather than aggressive, policy.'[22]

Interestingly enough, this open, if qualified, Soviet gesture towards Israel met with tacit approval from Damascus, thereby underlining the common Soviet-Syrian interest in containing the crisis. For in no way did Asad's readiness to challenge Israel in Lebanon imply a willingness to risk an armed clash. Rather, it resulted from a combination of Syria's reluctance to see the strategically located town of Zahla taken over by the Israeli-backed Phalanges militia, and Asad's growing self-confidence following the significant diminution of the domestic challenge to his regime. Since he believed Syria's military power to be still inferior to Israel's, Asad knew that the crisis could serve Syrian interests only as long as it did not slide into open hostilities.[23] This assumption proved to be accurate.

As the risk of a conflagration subsided, following the shift of Israeli attention from the Syrian missiles to other issues, particularly the destruction of the Iraqi nuclear reactor on 7 June 1981 and the confrontation with the PLO in southern Lebanon, Damascus emerged from the 'missile crisis' as the undisputed winner. By openly challenging Israel, Syria managed to appear as the bastion of the Arab cause, stepping out – albeit temporarily – from its regional isolation. On 22 May 1981, a conference of Arab foreign ministers, convened in Tunis at the request of Algeria and the PLO, promised Syria all necessary financial and military support to face the 'Israeli aggression'. No less important was Syria's success in changing the rules of the 'Lebanese game' in its favour without incurring any retaliation. By leaving the missiles in Lebanon, Syria not only reaped a propaganda victory and imposed a severe constraint on the Israeli air force's operational capabilities, but also improved its standing in the intra-Lebanese conflict.

In these circumstances, and notwithstanding its differences with the USSR on the relevance of the Friendship and Cooperation Treaty to the crisis, Damascus did not fail to praise Moscow's 'clear and firm stand', which, in its view, had helped to prevent an Israeli aggression.[24] Thus, according to Asad, 'the Soviet Union supports us against aggression. It is convinced that aggression is being committed against us. For this reason it supports us, aids us politically and supplies us.'[25] And the Syrian Minister of State for Foreign Affairs, Farouq Al-Shara, went a step further in depicting Soviet aid. 'Syria has tremendous Soviet support,' he stated in an interview with the London-based Arab journal, *Al-Majalah*, 'especially in that the Soviets will certainly not allow Syria to be defeated militarily.'[26]

Prelude to war
If Soviet support during the 'missile crisis' had been viewed by Syria as highly satisfactory, the rapidly changing circumstances of the

Arab-Israeli conflict were soon to restore Syria's sense of vulnerability, driving it to demand more visible proof of the USSR's
determination 'not to allow Syria to be defeated militarily'. In
September 1981, Menachem Begin journeyed to Washington, where
he managed to extract an American promise to sign a bilateral
agreement on strategic cooperation; the actual conclusion of the
agreement, known as the Memorandum of Strategic Understanding,
took place on 30 November, during a visit to the United States by
the Israeli Minister of Defence, Ariel Sharon.

The American-Israeli memorandum was received by Syria with
considerable alarm. 'To confirm its hostility to the Arabs, the United
States has entered into a strategic alliance with Israel, which includes
its obligation to defend 'Israeli security' against forces hostile to
Israel,' argued *Al-Ba'th* on 13 September, and 'since the Arab nation
is the major and only party in conflict with the Zionist entity, the US
pledge therefore means a declaration of war on the Arabs.' As the
Soviet-Syrian Treaty of Friendship and Cooperation – being a
purely defensive agreement – could not match the American-Israeli
'treaty of aggression',[27] there was now a pressing need for a
'qualitative leap in Soviet-Syrian relations'.[28]

By way of achieving this 'qualitative leap' a high-ranking Syrian
delegation, headed by the Minister of Defence, Mustafa Tlas, landed
in Moscow in mid-September, only to be bitterly disappointed.
Though obviously satisfied with the fresh eruption of anti-American
sentiment following the conclusion of the memorandum, and eager
to exploit this development to further discredit America's regional
role, the Soviets turned a deaf ear both to Tlas's request to elevate
the Friendship and Cooperation Treaty to a strategic alliance, and
to his pleas for increased supplies of sophisticated weaponry.[29]
Moreover, on 25 September, four days before meeting Abd Al-
Khalim Khaddam at the UN General Assembly, Andrei Gromyko
conferred with his Israeli counterpart, Yitzhak Shamir, in New
York, in an attempt to convince Israel to support the Soviet effort to
convene an international conference on the Middle East.[30]

Apart from indicating the Soviet interest in mending fences with
Jerusalem, Moscow's ability to court Israel at the time when it was
turning down desperate Syrian appeals for closer alignment and
increased military support demonstrated the fundamental improvement in the Soviet bargaining position *vis-à-vis* Damascus, dating
back to the Egyptian-Israeli peace process of late 1977. The Shamir-

Gromyko meeting, the first of its type in six years, constituted an unmistakable reminder to Syria that the ultimate say regarding the nature of the response to the new American-Israeli challenge lay with Moscow.

If there remained any doubts about Moscow's determination not to be swept by the tide of events in the direction of a defence pact with Syria, they were completely dispelled by the Soviet reaction to the Israeli annexation of the Golan Heights on 14 December 1981. Unlike Syria, which viewed the Israeli action as a public humiliation and a fundamental setback, the Soviet Union saw gains as well as losses in this latest development. In the first place, Damascus's heightened sense of insecurity following the Israeli action strengthened the USSR's bargaining position *vis-à-vis* Syria. Second, coming at the same time as the imposition of martial law in Poland, the extension of Israeli jurisdiction and law to the Golan Heights provided the Soviets with an opportunity to divert world public opinion from the events in Poland by unleashing a fresh propaganda campaign against the United States, which, so they claimed, bore the major responsibility for the Israeli move.[31] The fact that Washington responded to the annexation of the Golan Heights by suspending the Memorandum of Strategic Understanding, as well as by imposing a partial arms embargo on Israel, did nothing to alleviate the intensity of Soviet attacks on the United States.

The USSR did not, of course, rejoice at the temporary *rapprochement* between the United States and Syria, as Damascus expressed its satisfaction with American support for the UN Security Council Resolution 497 of 17 December 1981, which deplored the Israeli annexation and called upon Israel to nullify its decision.[32] But since this warming of relations turned out to be a very brief episode (in late January 1982 the United States vetoed a follow-up Security Council resolution on sanctions against Israel, and, in consequence, Syria resumed its harsh attacks on America's Middle East policy), the Soviets did not find it difficult to brush aside renewed Syrian requests for a defence pact, made during Khaddam's visit to Moscow on 14–15 January 1982.[33] And as if to signal to Damascus the advantages of the Friendship and Cooperation Treaty so as to forestall future requests for a defence pact, the Soviets stressed the importance of this treaty to Syrian security.

In contrast with the missile crisis, when Damascus had gained the upper hand, Syria's inability to find an adequate response to the annexation of the Golan Heights unequivocally exposed its inherent weakness *vis-à-vis* Israel. Since the United States had blocked the imposition of UN sanctions on Israel, Syria was left with only one option that would restore its dignity – the conclusion of a defence pact with the USSR.

Another hypothetical alternative – to resort to arms – was out of the question, given Syria's military inferiority *vis-à-vis* Israel. Indeed, despite defining the Israeli annexation of the Golan Heights as a 'declaration of war on Syria and cancellation of the 1973 ceasefire',[34] Syria took great care to clarify that it still abided by the provisions of the May 1974 disengagement agreement with Israel.[35] Moreover, in February 1982 Asad delivered a message to Israel through an informal channel he often used – Radio Monte Carlo's Damascus correspondent, Louis Farres – in which he expressed Syria's reluctance to clash militarily with Israel in Lebanon, and informed the Israeli leadership of Syria's 'threshold of tolerance' regarding a possible Israeli intervention in that country. 'If the Israeli intervention takes the form of strikes against Palestinian positions and camps in Lebanon,' read the note, 'Syria's intervention will remain limited.' However:

> If it is a matter of occupation, Syria will certainly give the Palestinians and the Lebanese patriotic forces all the means necessary for checking the occupation and turning the occupiers' life into unbearable hell, and this in addition to conducting the battles that will be called for in a time of need. It is no secret that Israel's military force is now larger than Syria's; therefore the possibility of Syria's turning to a full-scale war at a time and place determined by Israel should be excluded ... The activity will be limited to resistance to the occupation and to the attrition of the occupying forces ... but might develop into an all-out war if circumstances so determined.[36]

Paradoxically, this message played into the hands of the Israeli Minister of Defence, Ariel Sharon, by providing him with proof that his plan for a large-scale campaign against the Palestinian forces in Lebanon would not lead to a Syrian-Israeli confrontation. Whether and to what extent Sharon did use the Syrian message as a means to overcome opposition to his plan is difficult to tell. It is clear, however, that the Syrian communication did nothing to deter Israel. On 6 June

1982, Israeli forces crossed the Lebanese border in force, thereby putting the Soviet-Syrian bilateral treaty to its most severe test ever.

War over Lebanon

Neither the USSR nor Syria were wholly taken by surprise by the Israeli invasion of Lebanon. Given Israel's long-standing resistance to any form of direct Syrian military presence in Lebanon, Syria's growing interference in the Lebanese crisis from late 1975 onwards could not but contain the seeds of an armed confrontation between the two countries. Yet, since Israel and Syria found themselves in the same boat, with both reluctant to see a leftist-Palestinian victory, a tacit agreement was reached as early as 1976 on the 'rules of the game' in Lebanon. These rules were maintained, by and large, despite the fact that in 1977 Syria resumed its support for the PLO and turned against the Christian camp. Within this framework, Syria remained aloof at the time of the massive Israeli operation against the Palestinian forces in south Lebanon ('Operation Litani') in March 1978, thereby exposing itself to severe criticism from its opponents in the Arab world, particularly Iraq. Similarly, the air clashes between Syrian and Israeli aircraft over Lebanon in June and September 1979 did not result in a breakdown of the *modus vivendi* between these two arch-enemies.

This situation began to change in late 1980, when Begin promised the Phalangists that Israel would guarantee the security of the Lebanese Christian community. Encouraged by this far-reaching pledge, which included the provision of an Israeli aerial umbrella in case of Syrian air strikes against the Phalangist forces, the leader of the Christian militia, Bashir Gumayel, escalated his activities against the Syrian forces in Lebanon. By April 1981, the Phalangists' provocations had resulted in Syria laying siege to Zahla; from that point on, the road to the missile crisis, which brought Israel and Syria close to war, was short. Nor did the abating of the crisis in June 1981 eliminate the danger of war. With Begin still committed to the destruction of the surface-to-air missiles in Lebanon, and Defence Minister Sharon determined to overwhelm the Syrian forces in Lebanon during his envisaged campaign against the Palestinians – despite his public claims to the contrary[37] – the spectre of a Syrian-Israeli confrontation in Lebanon loomed large.

The escalation did not escape the Soviets' notice. Viewing Begin's second government as a 'government of war', which would sooner or later attack the Palestinian organizations in Lebanon, from late 1981 onwards the Soviet media repeatedly warned of Israel's intention to strike at Lebanon, intensifying these cautions during the winter of 1981 and the spring of 1982. On 1 March 1982, for example, a *Tass* commentary argued that the US Defence Secretary, Caspar Weinberger, 'practically gave the "green light" to Israeli intervention in Lebanon', and on 14 April *Izvestiya* accused Israel not only of unleashing 'bloody terror against the Palestinians on the West Bank and in the Gaza Strip', but also of 'preparing to crush Lebanon with its mailed fist' in order to 'strip the Palestinian people of their national rights' and to bring about their 'physical annihilation'. An official *Tass* statement, issued a week later in response to Israeli air strikes against the PLO, was no less strident: 'The Israeli air raid against Lebanon is strongly condemned by the Soviet Union, and the Soviet Union believes that the UN Security Council should, at long last, adopt effective measures to call the high-handed aggressor to order.'[38]

Moreover, once war broke out, the Soviets were quick to dismiss Israel's justification of its invasion and to point perceptively to the real motives behind it. 'Begin indicated that the Israeli army has been ordered to push the Palestinians 25 miles from the border,' said *Izvestiya*'s political commentator, Alexander Bovin, but in fact, he argued, Israel had other, more far-reaching aims:

Tel Aviv's first aim is to destroy the military infrastructure of the PLO, smash its military formation and thereby greatly weaken its role and significance. According to Tel Aviv's schemes this should prepare the ground for the second stage of the Camp David process. It is estimated that, on the one hand, a weakened and intimidated Lebanon will agree to conclude a separate agreement with Israel along the lines of the Camp David set-up, while, on the other hand, the weakening of the PLO should push Jordan into joining the Camp David process ... Second, Tel Aviv is quite obviously pursuing the aim of forcing Syria out of Lebanon and thus increasing its isolation.[39]

It is exactly this keen awareness of Israeli intentions which has left many observers of Soviet Middle East policy perplexed, if not disappointed, with the level of Soviet engagement in the 1982 Lebanon War. 'The Soviet Union may have some questions to answer from its friends and allies in the Middle East at the close of the current crisis in Lebanon,' wrote one commentator. 'Given the massive material and political support Moscow had accorded both Syria and the Palestinian Liberation Organization in the past, it is possible that they, or at least groups among their supporters and the public at large, expected something more than the virtual inaction of the Soviet Union.'[40] Extending this line of reasoning, many explanations were offered for Moscow's 'virtual inaction'; these ranged from logistical difficulties in the provision of military support to a succession crisis in the Soviet leadership, to external considerations and constraints (e.g., the crises in Poland and Afghanistan, and strategic arms negotiations).[41]

While giving a fairly accurate account of Moscow's support for the PLO, these views do a great injustice to its behaviour towards Syria. For both during the period of active fighting between Israel and Syria (6–25 June 1982), and in its aftermath, Moscow extended the same military and political support to Damascus as it had done in previous Arab-Israeli wars. Furthermore, its military support consisted of the same ingredients as before: namely, arms shipments, modest advisory assistance, a naval show of force, as well as the alerting of airborne units in the USSR.

The only difference between Soviet activities during the 1982 War and on previous occasions, therefore, is one of degree – a difference that derives from the limited nature of the Lebanon War. Unlike the October War, which involved the entire Syrian and Egyptian armed forces, only one third of the Syrian army (two out of six divisions) took part in the 1982 War. Consequently, and given the impressive build-up of the Syrian armed forces between 1979 and 1982, Syria's losses appeared negligible. For example, in the Lebanon War the Syrians lost only 10 per cent of their tanks (400 out of 4,000), compared with 66 per cent in the October War (1,000 out of 1,500). Even in the aerial and air defence fields, where Syria suffered the most telling blows, the losses did not resemble those of the 1973 war: 20 per cent in surface-to-air missile batteries (20 out of 100) and 15 per cent in combat aircraft (90 out of 600), compared with 50 per cent and 65 per cent respectively.

Syria's ability to sustain the war losses made the question of wartime resupply far less acute than in the October War. In fact, the most critical losses were already compensated for during the course of hostilities: by 10 June, four days after the onset of hostilities, a modest Soviet airlift, consisting of three or four daily flights by IL-76 transport aircraft, was already delivering to Syria surface-to-air missiles and crated planes. Seaborne arms began arriving a week later, with six merchant ships reported to have unloaded military equipment – including tanks, armoured vehicles and surface-to-air missiles – at Syrian ports.[42] Soviet arms transfers were significantly accelerated immediately after the war, and within a short time all Syria's war losses had been replaced.

Since Soviet advisers had strictly avoided taking permanent positions within the Syrian forces deployed in Lebanon, no Soviet personnel were engaged in the ground fighting. Consequently, Soviet advisory support was limited to the aerial and air-defence fields outside Lebanese territory. On 13 June, this involvement was highlighted by the arrival in Damascus of a Soviet military delegation, headed by General Yevgeny Yurasov, First Deputy Commander-in-Chief of the Soviet Air Defence Forces. Besides attending an official meeting with the Syrian minister of defence, the Soviet delegation held several working sessions with their Syrian counterparts, discussing ways and means of countering the challenge posed by the Israeli air force.[43] Within a few days of Yurasov's departure the Soviets were reported to have delivered to Syria a number of SA-8 missile batteries and to have employed them (from Syrian territory) against the Israeli air force.[44]

At the same time the Soviet Mediterranean Squadron was enlarged by nine ships (bringing the total to 39), and a naval task-force was deployed in the eastern Mediterranean, thus placing some combatants in immediate proximity to the battle zone. During this period there was also a significant growth in the volume of communications between Soviet airborne divisions. The exact nature of this exceptional activity, as well as the reason for its occurrence, was not entirely clear; but there was evidence that at least one airborne division was placed on alert.[45]

In the political sphere, the Soviets aimed at mobilizing the widest possible support for the Arab cause and bringing the maximum pressure to bear upon Israel. A major arena for Soviet activity was the United Nations, where the USSR laboriously sought to arrange a Security Council resolution that would contain the Israeli campaign. The subsequent American vetoes on such resolutions were presented by the Soviets as proof of US-Israeli collusion and sufficient reason for Arab economic retaliation against the United States, by means of an oil embargo and the withdrawal of petro-dollar funds from American banks.[46]

A no less important channel for the Soviet Union throughout the war was its direct communication with the American administration, which included several messages sent from Brezhnev to Reagan. As early as 10 June the Soviet leader forwarded an urgent message to Reagan, which apparently contained an implied and subtle threat of Soviet intervention, should the war assume more menacing proportions.[47] Though it is difficult to ascertain the exact impact of the Soviet note – President Reagan was reported to have responded by cautioning Brezhnev not to contemplate any intervention[48] – it may have strengthened the case of those within the administration who supported the restraint of Israel; indeed, on 11 June Israel gave in to American pressures to accept a ceasefire.

Moscow's diplomatic activity was supplemented by a vocal propaganda campaign, intended to deter Israel by indicating the grave consequences of its 'aggression'. As early as 7 June, a day after the onset of hostilities, *Tass* issued its first official statement regarding the war. Condemning the Israeli invasion of Lebanon, the statement warned Israel that the continuation of its campaign was 'an adventure which may cost Israel dear'.[49] A week later, as Israeli forces, in disregard of the 11 June ceasefire agreement, arrived at the outskirts of Beirut and appeared to be on the verge of driving the Syrians out of the Beq'a valley, the Soviet government issued a more strongly worded official statement:

Israel is committing a criminal act of genocide in Lebanon. Sparing no one, the troops of the aggressor are virtually annihilating the Palestinians to a man, and thousands of Lebanese are also dying ... The action by Israel and its patrons also poses a threat to other Arab states. The same old line of subordinating the Arab countries, one by one, to the imperialist dictates is clear ... *The Soviet Union takes the side of the Arabs, not in words but in deeds*. It is working to bring about the withdrawal of the aggressor from Lebanon. *Those who now direct Israeli policy should not forget that the Middle East is situated in close proximity to the southern borders of the Soviet Union, and events there cannot fail to affect the interests of the USSR. We warn Israel about this.*[50]

As is well known, neither the Soviet warnings nor the military actions that accompanied them had a direct impact on Israel. The second Syrian-Israeli ceasefire, which came into effect on 25 June and terminated the war between the two countries, resulted from both American pressures and the attainment of Israel's operational objectives (i.e., the securing of the Beirut-Damascus highway and the resulting control of Beirut).

If Moscow's political and military activities on behalf of the Arab cause did have any impact, it was of an indirect and elusive nature: namely, the injection of a greater sense of urgency into the American decision-making process. But this does not imply 'virtual inaction' on the Soviets' part, for it was through the American channel that the USSR had attempted to influence the outcome of previous Arab-Israeli wars, with varying degrees of success. Given Moscow's commitment to the Arab cause from the mid-1950s onwards, on the one hand, and Israel's military supremacy over its Arab neighbours, on the other, there was little the Soviets could do to save their allies from defeat but put presure on the United States to restrain Israel. Thus Soviet threats of military intervention in the 1956, 1967 and 1973 wars were effective only to the extent of prompting the United States to pressure Israel to halt its advance.[51]

Moreover, both the territorial confinement of the 1982 War and Syria's relatively limited involvement in it excluded from the outset the possibility of, and the need for, direct Soviet intervention on behalf of Syria. Fighting Israel on Lebanese territory, Damascus had no legal grounds to request the dispatch of Soviet forces, particularly since Israel was not at war with Lebanon, and the latter, maintaining a traditionally pro-Western orientation, was most unlikely to request Soviet support. Even if there was some truth in Israeli intelligence reports about the existence of a Soviet undertaking to send troops to Syria, should the regime there be in imminent danger[52] – and there are no indications that a formal pledge to this effect was made – such an agreement could hardly be invoked in the circumstances of the 1982 War, which took place outside Syrian territory, involved a small portion of Syria's armed forces and thus fell short of posing a serious threat to the Asad regime.

Consequently, Moscow did not have 'some questions to answer' from its Syrian friends. Unlike the PLO, whose military infrastructure in Lebanon suffered a mortal blow, Syria could – and did – take some pride in its combat performance. Its position in Lebanon deteriorated following its limited defeat on the ground and the public humiliation attending its unmatched losses in the aerial and air defence fields. Yet Syria's success in frustrating the Israeli campaign, and, moreover, in attaining this objective alone, without proper air cover and in the face of Israel's overwhelming numerical superiority on the ground, was considered a significant achievement by the regime in Damascus. Thus, while the PLO was quick to express its frustration over the lack of Soviet support, Syria had nothing but praise for the Soviet Union. For example, a statement on the military situation, issued on 19 June by the Progressive National Front, referred to the Soviet Union as 'the loyal friend of our people and nation and the strong supporter of our struggle and right'.[53] Similarly, the Syrian government, in its meeting on 21 June, 'emphasized that the deep and strong cooperation between Syria and the USSR, which is a permanent base of the struggle against the powers of aggression ... would remain a constant basis that gives the battle between the Arabs, on one side, and America and Israel, on the other, its real scope in this region and everywhere else.'[54]

Its satisfaction with Moscow's role during the 1982 War notwithstanding, Damascus sought to exploit the events in Lebanon in order to gain a greater Soviet commitment to Syrian security, in the form of both extended military supplies and, if possible, the elevation of the 1980 treaty into a bilateral defence pact.[55] The Syrian efforts to mobilize greater Soviet support, which included a secret – and highly important – visit paid by Asad to Moscow in late June, were largely successful. The Soviet Union was anxious to eliminate Israel's (and, more so, America's) presence and influence in Lebanon, on the one hand, and to undermine the Reagan peace plan of 1 September 1982,[56] on the other; and Syria was the only actor capable of achieving these goals. Moreover, by destroying twenty Syrian surface-to-air missile batteries and shooting down some ninety of Syria's frontline interceptor aircraft without suffering a single casualty, the Israeli air force had exposed the weakness of the Soviet-type air defence system, dealing yet another painful blow at the reputation of the Soviet weaponry. Given the USSR's reliance on much the same systems for the defence of its own airspace, a prompt response to the challenge posed by Israel became not only a matter of recovering lost prestige, but also a pressing operational need.[57]

Consequently, while turning down the idea of a defence pact and taking care not to link the Friendship and Cooperation Treaty to the crisis in Lebanon, the Soviets were responsive to Asad's requests in several crucial respects. First, just as Nasser's famous visit to

Moscow in January 1970 resulted in the deployment of an extensive Soviet air defence system in Egypt, so Asad's visit culminated in the decision to restore the 'lost honour' of Syria's air defence system by deploying Soviet-manned SAM-5 surface-to-air missiles in Syria.[58] Second, not only did the Soviets agree to replace Syria's war losses, but they apparently acquiesced in Asad's request to back the further expansion of the Syrian armed forces; this acquiescence manifested itself in $2.8 billion worth of weapons supplied to Syria between June 1982 and early 1984. Finally, Moscow recognized Syria's role in Lebanon, and declared its readiness to support Damascus in attempts to drive the Israeli (and American) forces out of that country – attempts which made extensive use of brinkmanship tactics, threatening on more than one occasion to slide into open confrontation between Syria and Israel.

Although Moscow's support for the Syrian anti-Israel campaign in Lebanon did not imply, at least during Brezhnev's last months, any willingness to go beyond the already established pattern of arms supplies and political backing, Moscow's forthcoming approach was immediately reciprocated by Syria. Although he sent Foreign Minister Khaddam to Washington in early July 1982 to explore, with his Saudi counterpart, the possibility of American pressures on Israel, Asad's view of America's Middle Eastern role remained negative. Considering the United States the motivating force behind Israel's invasion of Lebanon, Asad willingly joined Soviet attempts to foil the American policy. Apart from supporting Brezhnev's initiative of 21 July to convene an international conference on the Middle East,[59] Syria conducted a fierce campaign against the Reagan Plan from its very announcement, playing a decisive role in its ultimate failure. Thus, at the Fez summit of Arab leaders in September 1982, Syria obstructed Saudi attempts to bridge the gap between the Reagan Plan and the Arab position on a settlement. Similarly, Syria exploited its participation in the seven-member committee, which travelled to several capitals (including Washington), as a means to explain the Fez decisions and thus to forestall any deviation from the Fez peace plan.

In November 1982, however, Brezhnev died, leaving his successor, Yuri Andropov, to bring Soviet-Syrian cooperation to its peak.

6

FROM BREZHNEV
TO GORBACHEV

Upon his accession to power in mid-November 1982, Yuri Andropov was confronted with two interconnected adverse ramifications of the 1982 War: on the one hand, the Israeli and American forces in Lebanon and the resultant pressure on the Lebanese regime to conclude a separate peace treaty with Israel, and, on the other, America's efforts to bring about a comprehensive Arab-Israeli settlement along the lines of the Reagan Plan. In order to overcome these problems, Andropov moved resolutely and swiftly along his predecessor's path. Having concluded a new large-scale arms deal with Syria as early as November 1982,[1] he rapidly carried out Brezhnev's pledge (given during Asad's visit to Moscow in late June 1982) to dispatch Soviet air defence units to Syria: in late 1982 Israeli and American intelligence services detected preparations for the installation of two SAM-5 surface-to-air missile brigades in Syria, and by January 1983 these units had already been deployed in the Damascus and Homs areas.

The unprecedented deployment of SAM-5s in Syria – the first time that such missiles had been deployed outside the Soviet Union – was accompanied by Soviet warnings to Israel not to take any military action against Syria, backed by hints of the USSR's willingness to intervene on Syria's behalf (though not on Lebanese territory),[2] should Syria be subjected to an Israeli attack: 'The Soviet Union and Syria are linked by a Treaty of Friendship and Cooperation, which is considered the basis of the relations between the two countries. It is essential that all this must not be forgotten by those who threaten to use arms . . .'[3] Whether or not the Soviet warnings had any restraining impact on Israel, they certainly enhanced Syria's self-confidence.[4] Encouraged by the massive flow of arms, the vocal Soviet support and the growing war-weariness in Israel, Syria launched a two-pronged campaign to frustrate the Reagan Plan and any Lebanese-Israeli peace treaty.

In the autumn of 1982, Syria communicated to the US administration – and through it to Israel – its categorical refusal to withdraw its troops from Lebanon before all foreign troops had been evacuated. 'We want Lebanon to have accord and security now, and we want its legitimate authority to assume full control of all of Lebanon,' Asad told a US congressional delegation in November 1982; therefore, 'when the Israeli occupation is removed from Lebanon we will not make any conditions for our withdrawal.' 'However,' he added, 'if Lebanon needed our presence before the Israeli invasion, then its need now is more urgent.'[5]

Oddly enough, the Syrian message passed unheeded. The administration, assuming that the various constraints on Syria's continued presence in Lebanon (e.g., the cost, the threat of a Syrian-Israeli confrontation) would eventually force Damascus to modify its position on the question of withdrawal, decided to strive for a separate Lebanese-Israeli agreement which would present the Syrians with a *fait accompli*. But the administration failed to take into account either the intensity of Syria's long-standing interest in Lebanon or the extent of Syrian influence there. Instead of moderating Syrian hostility, the US strategy triggered a relentless Syrian campaign against a separate Lebanese-Israeli deal. This was conducted on several levels, ranging from heavy pressures on the Lebanese president, Amin Gumayel, to avoid any concessions to Israel, to material support for Gumayel's opponents (particularly the Lebanese Druse), to the significant reinforcement of the Syrian forces in Lebanon to the unprecedented and menacing level of 1,200 tanks.[6]

The consolidation of Syria's military presence in Lebanon, was detrimental not only to the evolution of the American-inspired Lebanese-Israeli dialogue, but also to the viability of the Reagan Plan. Wishing to exploit Syria's strong position in Lebanon, Asad linked the Reagan Plan to the developments there, portraying these as part of an American-Israeli attempt to impose a 'second Camp David' on the Arabs. Moreover, when in October 1982 the PLO leader, Yasser Arafat, decided to enter into negotiations with King Hussein on the possibility of a joint Jordanian-Palestinian delegation in peace talks based on the Reagan Plan, Asad began to make life difficult for Arafat's organization, Al-Fath – the largest of all PLO constituent organizations.

Combined with a skilful manipulation of the pro-Syrian constituent organizations of the PLO, as well as with a political propaganda campaign, the Syrian pressure bore immediate fruit: in mid-February 1983 the Palestine National Council (PNC) convened in Algiers for its 16th session and categorically rejected the suitability of the Reagan Plan as a basis for the solution of the Palestinian problem. True, the PNC left the door open for further contacts between Arafat and King Hussein. But the highly restricted framework within which Arafat was allowed to act doomed the Jordanian-Palestinian negotiations. On 10 April 1983 the frustrated and impatient Jordanian government issued a communiqué admitting the collapse of the Jordanian-Palestinian dialogue and putting the blame on the PLO.

Since it implied the *de facto* collapse of the Reagan Plan, the Jordanian announcement was received with deep satisfaction in both Damascus and Moscow. Like Syria, the USSR had been worried by the possibility of the PLO being integrated into the Reagan peace initiative. Thus, while it avoided direct criticism of the PLO leadership, Moscow voiced subtle expressions of Soviet dissatisfaction with Arafat's moves, as well as support for Syria's position on the Jordanian-Palestinian negotiations. For example, a *Selskaya Zhizn* article on 22 January 1983 contained severe criticism of those who were trying to 'link up that anti-Arab plan [i.e., the Reagan Plan] and the plan approved by the Arab heads of state and government in Fez'. Similarly, in a meeting with Farouq Kadoumi in November 1982, the Soviet Foreign Minister, Andrei Gromyko, urged the PLO to increase its cooperation with 'the national patriotic forces of the Arab world, above all, with Syria, which resolutely opposes the plans of the aggressors.'[7] Two months later, in January 1983, an equally urgent request for the PLO to mend its fences with Damascus was reportedly addressed to Yasser Arafat by Andropov in person, during their meeting in Moscow.[8]

Perhaps its most significant service to the Soviet Union since the (temporary) obstruction of the Egyptian-Israeli disengagement talks in early 1975, Syria's undermining of the Reagan Plan was not matched by success on the Lebanese front: on 17 May 1983 Israel signed its second peace treaty with an Arab country – Lebanon. Yet the celebrated American-Israeli achievement turned out to be a Pyrrhic victory: Syria's uncompromising rejection soon rendered it inoperative.

Fully aware that Syria could wreck the treaty by not evacuating its forces from Lebanon, Asad embarked upon a determined effort to forge the Lebanese forces opposed to it into a unified front. This goal was attained in late July 1983 with the establishment of the 'National Salvation Front', an organization linking seven parties, headed by the Druse leader Walid Jumblatt and the Shi'ite leader Nabih Berri, together with the leading politicians Rashid Karami and Suleiman Faranjieh. The formation of the Front was accompanied by heavy pressure on the Lebanese government, which intensified considerably following the unilateral evacuation of Israeli forces from the Shouf Mountains in early September 1983 and the seizure of these strategic mountains by the Syrians and the Lebanese.

Syria's vigorous campaign was followed by the Soviet Union with mixed feelings. To be sure, Moscow was as keen as Damascus to obstruct the Lebanese-Israeli agreement, since the successful implementation of the American-sponsored arrangement could once more leave the USSR on the sidelines, whereas its collapse would mean a boost to the USSR's prestige and a humiliating blow to its rival superpower. Indications of a renaissance in Moscow's regional standing were seen that summer, when the US administration, in disregard of its commitment to exclude the Soviets from negotiations on the withdrawal of foreign forces from Lebanon, approached the USSR on several occasions, asking it to use its good offices in Damascus.[9]

Yet despite the substantial advantages to be gained from Damascus's relentless campaign, the Soviets had three main reasons for unease. First, Syria's struggle to destroy the Lebanese-Israeli agreement brought it (or so it appeared at the time) to the verge of war with Israel. Relying on war-weariness in Israel to prevent a second round of fighting in Lebanon, Asad resorted to his notorious brinkmanship tactics, allowing pro-Syrian terrorist groups to operate from Syrian-controlled Lebanese territory against Israeli targets, and even initiating sporadic direct clashes with the Israeli Defence Forces (IDF). In May 1983 the two countries came closer than ever to full confrontation when, in response to Syrian threats and alarming moves (e.g., large-scale manoeuvres on the Golan Heights, call-up of reservists), Israel put some of its units on a higher state of alert and declared a partial mobilization.

The second cause of concern was the growing tension between Syria and its Lebanese supporters, on the one hand, and the Western – particularly US – forces stationed in Beirut, on the other. True, the spectre of such a confrontation was not entirely unwelcome to the Soviets, since it would seriously challenge the American military presence in Lebanon (a goal that Moscow was unable to attain on its own) and give the USSR a useful weapon against US Middle Eastern policy. But the risk that escalation would follow a direct Syrian-American encounter was too great. After the occupation of the Shouf, as Druse and Shi'ite military pressure on the Lebanese government intensified, the US Marines in Beirut came under increasingly heavy fire, and on 23 October a suicide truck-bomb destroyed their headquarters in Beirut. American retaliation, in the form of heavy naval shelling of Syrian and Druse positions in the Shouf, as well as air-strikes on Syrian strongholds in the Beq'a, did little to moderate Syria's bellicose stance.[10]

Finally. Moscow was concerned at the heavy pressure Syria was putting on the PLO in its effort to undermine Arafat's leadership and to make the weakened organization subservient to its own wishes. As during the 1976 Lebanese crisis, the growing conflict between Syria and the PLO was highly inconvenient for the Soviets, forcing them to tread cautiously between two of their most prized Middle Eastern allies. By June 1983 the Syrian pressure had produced an armed revolt against Arafat's authority by pro-Syrian elements within Al-Fath, headed by Abu Musa. Though the Syrians vehemently denied any responsibility for the internal strife within Al-Fath, it was evident that the rebellion in the Syrian-controlled Beq'a could not have taken place without Damascus's approval. Indeed, as the year neared its end, Syria's involvement in the revolt became more than evident: having driven Arafat's loyalists out of the Beq'a to the Tripoli area, and ultimately into the city itself, in mid-November Syrian-backed units laid siege to Tripoli; a month later, a humiliating evacuation of PLO forces from Lebanon took place – the second that year, though this time from Tripoli, rather than from Beirut, and under Syrian, rather than Israeli, pressure.

Given this amalgam of risks and opportunities, Moscow's anxiety to undermine the American-Israeli position in Lebanon, and its interest in keeping its relationship with Syria intact, came to outweigh the fears of escalation. Flatly rejecting American appeals to restrain Syria, and ensuring that this rejection received due publicity,[11] Moscow justified Syria's uncompromising drive against the agreement of 17 May, which ran 'counter to the independence of Lebanon and its freedom and interests, as well as the security of Syria and its interests'.[12] As the only obstacle to the transformation of Lebanon into a 'springboard for aggressive actions against neighbouring Arab states',[13] the Syrian position was bound to incur the wrath of the American-Israeli axis. However, the United States and Israel should keep in mind two fundamental facts: first, that 'Syria has an adequate defence potential to repel aggression'; second, that Syria did not stand alone 'in the Arab world or the international arena in general', for 'the Soviet Union will continue to support the struggle of the Syrian, Lebanese, Palestinian and other Arab peoples against the aggressive schemes of the USA and Israel.'[14] This pledge of support was accompanied by concrete demonstrations of backing, such as the visit of the aircraft carrier *Novosibirsk* to Tartus in late June, and, more important, the delivery of the advanced SS-21 surface-to-surface missiles to the Syrian army in October – the first delivery of this kind to a local ally.[15]

Another important facet of Moscow's support for Syria's Lebanese policy was the Soviet position *vis-à-vis* the deepening breach between Damascus and the PLO leadership. Already in late 1982 the USSR's disenchantment with Arafat's 'flirting' with King Hussein led it to support Syria in its feud with the PLO. Similarly, the USSR had little difficulty in making up its mind with which party to side in the renewed confrontation between Asad and Arafat in the summer of 1983. In June, for example, when Syrian-Palestinian relations were deteriorating fast, following the Abu Musa rebellion and Arafat's disgraceful expulsion from Damascus, it was the PLO, and not Syria, which incurred the lion's share of Soviet displeasure. In a series of messages to Arafat, Andropov reportedly urged him to do all he could to reach a *rapprochement* with Damascus, admitting the USSR's limited leverage over Syria. A month later, a scheduled visit by Arafat to the Soviet Union failed to materialize, thus indicating the poor status of the relations between Moscow and the PLO. When Farouq Kadoumi, instead of Arafat, arrived in the

Soviet capital in mid-July, he not only failed to obtain a Soviet agreement to mediate between the rival factions of the PLO, as well as between the PLO and Syria, but also was pressured to increase PLO cooperation with the 'progressive Arab countries'.[16]

Nor did Syria avoid a measure of Soviet pressure, as Moscow became increasingly convinced of the counter-productivity of the Syrian campaign against the PLO. Far from undermining Arafat's leadership or bringing the PLO under Syrian control (in itself an undesirable development from the Soviet point of view), Damascus – and Moscow – had to watch Arafat resume his flirtation with Jordan and, moreover, turn to Egypt in an attempt to gain protection against Syrian hostility.[17] However, the Soviet pressure on Syria posed no threat to the bilateral relationship; the Soviets continued to provide extensive shipments of arms to the Syrian armed forces, as well as staunch support for Damascus's campaign against the US and Israel. Furthermore, when in open defiance of a Soviet request (made during Khaddam's visit to Moscow on 10–11 November 1983) Syria launched a fresh offensive against the PLO forces in Tripoli, the USSR's criticism was confined to the call for a reconciliation between the PLO, 'the political vanguard of the Palestinian resistance', and Syria, 'which now is a most important force countering the aggressive plans of the USA and Israel'.[18]

Indeed, it was Moscow's keen awareness of Syria's 'most important role' which was at the root of the more daring and far-reaching Soviet backing of the Syrian campaign in Lebanon under Andropov. The relative salience of the Friendship and Cooperation Treaty throughout most stages of the crisis reflected this awareness: whereas during the various Syrian-Israeli crises of the late Brezhnev years the USSR went to great lengths to prevent any unwarranted interpretation of the commitments entailed in the bilateral treaty, shunning almost completely any reference to this accord,[19] Andropov was inclined to give the treaty a more generous interpretation. Though making it clear that Moscow's commitment to Syrian security in accordance with the treaty *did not* go beyond Syria's territory – more precisely, that this commitment did not extend to the Syrian forces in Lebanon – Andropov did not fail to imply that under the treaty the USSR felt itself obliged to come to Syria's aid in case of need.

'The Soviet-Syrian treaty has acquired particular significance in the present circumstances, with the imperialists constantly bringing pressure to bear upon Syria to make it change its steadfast Middle East policy,' wrote the Soviet weekly *New Times* on the third anniversary of the 1980 treaty. 'It is not easy, however, to undermine the Soviet-Syrian cooperation ... Year after year the Soviet-Syrian Treaty of Friendship and Cooperation serves as the basis for rebuffing the aggressive policy pursued by the imperialists and Zionists.'[20] And the joint communiqué issued at the close of Khaddam's visit to Moscow in November 1983 confirmed Moscow's 'adherence to the commitments under [the 1980] treaty'.[21]

Moscow's ardent aid and support for the Syrian venture in Lebanon bore abundant fruit. By the time of Andropov's death on 10 February 1984, Syria had generously repaid the Soviets. First, it had succeeded in dealing a mortal blow to the Reagan Plan in the spring of 1983. Second, through direct and indirect pressure on the US Marines in Beirut, it had managed to attain the much-coveted Soviet goal of driving the United States out of Lebanon: on 7 February 1984 Reagan announced his intention to withdraw the Marines from Beirut to US ships off the Lebanese coast, and within three weeks the evacuation had been completed. Finally, the relentless Syrian campaign against the American-sponsored Lebanese-Israeli agreement had led to the collapse of that arrangement: on 5 March 1984, in an attempt to save his shaky regime, President Amin Gumayel unilaterally abrogated the 17 May agreement with Israel.

During Andropov's brief period of leadership the Soviets also benefited from reinforced relations with Syria. In the political field, the Soviets drew comfort from Syria's support for both the Soviet peace plan and an international conference on the Middle East.[22] Contrary to the common view,[23] the fact that the USSR and Syria found themselves in opposing camps in the Gulf War, with the former aiding Iraq and the latter supporting Iran, did not damage their cooperation. Although it injected a measure of antagonism into the relationship, Syria's closeness to Iran provided a useful channel of communication between Moscow and Tehran. This channel assumed a special significance in 1983, when Soviet-Iranian relations reached their lowest ebb; indeed, during that year Syria was reported to have mediated (unsuccessfully) between the USSR and Iran.[24]

Benefits also followed in the economic field. In April 1983, for example, the two countries signed an agreement on the promotion of maritime and shipping cooperation which included the reciprocal granting of Most-Favoured-Nation (MFN) status.[25] A month earlier, Syria was reported to have given the Soviet Union, unexpectedly, a £120-million contract for a power station outside Damascus, already awarded to the Swedish company ASEA. Similarly, to the irritation of the Ministry of Transportation, Asad ordered the national airline to be re-equipped with TU-154 passenger jets, instead of the Boeing which constituted the backbone of the fleet at the time.[26]

Chernenko and the Syrians

Faced with the irksome task of restoring Moscow's regional standing, severely damaged during the 1982 War, Soviet Middle Eastern policy under Andropov became increasingly dependent on Syria's actions and, in consequence, almost exclusively concerned with events in Lebanon. Konstantin Chernenko was bequeathed a far more favourable political climate than his predecessor. With the US Marines (and other Western forces) banished from Lebanon, the Lebanese-Israeli agreement destroyed and the Reagan Plan tarnished, the new Secretary-General could gradually carry Soviet Middle Eastern policy out of the confines of Lebanon, thereby making it less dependent on Syrian action or inaction. In doing so, Chernenko could rely not only on the improvement of Moscow's regional position, which owed much to Syria's vigorous policy, but also on the domestic turmoil that broke out in Syria in late 1983. On 13 November Asad was unexpectedly hospitalized for what was later found to be a critical heart failure. This event triggered the first significant succession struggle within the Syrian leadership; the conflict was active until Asad's recovery in the spring of 1984 and remained latent until the end of that year.

From his earliest days in power, Chernenko embarked upon a campaign to widen Moscow's Middle Eastern horizons beyond the pro-Soviet 'radical' camp. He was helped in this by the return to power of the Israeli Labour Party in autumn 1984 (though in the framework of a National Unity government with the right-wing Likud Party), since the Labour Party had declared its readiness to negotiate a peace settlement with Jordan that involved territorial compromise on Israel's part. Hence the Soviet courtship of Jordan, illustrated both by the Jordanian Chief of Staff's visit to Moscow in August to discuss a new Soviet-Jordanian arms deal and by the

Soviet peace plan of 29 July 1984, which supported a confederation of the Hashemite Kingdom and the envisaged Palestinian state on the West Bank and in the Gaza Strip.[27] Hence, too, the Soviet efforts to make inroads into the 'conservative' Arab camp, leading to the resumption of full diplomatic relations with Egypt in July 1984. Equally irritating for the Syrians were Andrei Gromyko's meeting with Yasser Arafat in Berlin on 7 October (the first meeting between Arafat and a high-ranking Soviet official in nearly two years), the meeting between the Soviet and Israeli foreign ministers in New York during the United Nations General Assembly in September 1984, and the visit of the Iraqi Foreign Minister, Tariq Aziz, to Moscow in October 1984.

Asad not only disapproved of Chernenko's policy, but also began to doubt the USSR's readiness to maintain its extensive military support of Syria, which had been established following the 1982 Lebanon War. Moscow's generosity in the aftermath of the war was directly related to its anxiety to recover its regional standing following the Israeli action in Lebanon. Once Moscow's sense of vulnerability diminished as a result of the American-Israeli setbacks in Lebanon, Asad feared that the USSR would cut its supplies to Syria. Such fears must have been compounded by the view expressed in the Soviet media that Syria 'now has the defensive capability needed to protect its national independence and defend its political line'.[28]

A visit in March 1984 by Geidar Aliyev, a member of the Politburo and First Deputy Premier of the USSR, failed to reassure Asad, and in late May he sent his younger brother, Vice-President Rif'at Asad,[29] to Moscow, only to get first-hand proof of Moscow's less forthcoming approach to the issue of military support. While pledging to maintain 'unswerving support' for Syria's 'principled position', the Soviet leaders made it clear that this support did not necessarily relate to the military sphere, since in their view 'the Arabs possess all necessary means for foiling the schemes of US imperialism and its Israeli partners.'[30]

Asad was expecting far more from his major ally than expressions of support. On 15 October 1984 he arrived in Moscow for an official visit, the first of its kind since the historic October 1980 one during which the Friendship and Cooperation Treaty had been signed.[31] To judge by the exceptionally limited and low-key coverage given by the Soviet media to the visit, it was no more successful than Rif'at's talks in Moscow five months earlier. Not only did Asad fail to get the assurances he sought with regard to Moscow's attitude towards Jordan and Egypt, but the Soviets were reported to have tried to convince him to adopt a more lenient approach towards these countries, arguing that Jordan and Egypt (as well as Yasser Arafat) wanted a comprehensive, and not a separate, settlement.[32]. Two other bones of contention during the visit were related to the Syrian-PLO feud and the Iran-Iraq War. The Soviets reportedly emphasized the urgency of an Iraqi-Syrian reconciliation, pressurizing Asad to reopen pipelines carrying Iraqi oil to the Mediterranean terminal of Banias, which had been cut off in April 1982.[33]

On top of these differences on regional issues, Asad found his hosts cool on the bilateral level. True, he succeeded in extracting a Soviet agreement on increased economic and military aid to Syria,[34] but to Asad's obvious dismay, the Soviets took the exceptional step of linking their support for Syria with a willingness on Syria's part to assist 'other Arab nations in every way in their work for a just and lasting peace in the Middle East'.[35] This linkage was particularly galling for Syria, not only because it indicated the Soviets' determination to go ahead with a new arms deal with Jordan, whose relations with Syria were very poor at the time,[36] but also because it implied an erosion of Syria's position as Moscow's most prominent ally. Indeed, during the visit Asad was apparently informed by Chernenko of the latter's intention to withdraw the Soviet air defence units from Syria and to transfer the control of the SA-5 missiles to the Syrians. While this decision may be considered a Syrian achievement – the equipping of the Syrian armed forces with an important weapons system not previously under their direct control – it certainly reflected Moscow's decreasing readiness to take risks on Syria's behalf.[37]

Although the Syrians avoided direct criticism of the Soviet behaviour and portrayed Asad's visit to Moscow as a success, they soon gave the Soviets some subtle, but pointed, hints that their support should not be taken for granted. For example, the Foreign Minister, Farouq Al-Shara, expressed in a number of interviews his country's support for an American mediation effort, under the auspices of the UN, to end the Israeli occupation of Lebanon; in Al-Shara's view, the US administration had acknowledged its mistaken policy in Lebanon and had recognized Syria's central role in that region.[38]

Another attempt to assert Syrian independence came in the form of President François Mitterrand's visit to Damascus in late November 1984 – the first visit of a French president to Syria since its independence. Given that some eight years earlier, in June 1976, during the height of the Soviet-Syrian confrontation over Lebanon, Asad had journeyed to Paris for the first time in his presidency, the Syrian message to Moscow was unmistakable. And as if to dispel any remaining doubts among the Soviet decision-makers on this point, Syria publicized its intention to buy French, and perhaps other Western, arms.[39]

Whether or not the Soviets took seriously Syria's threat to diversify its weapons sources, the fast and unpredictable tide of Middle Eastern events was soon to bring the USSR and Syria closer again: on 22–29 November 1984 the Palestinian National Council convened in Amman for its 17th session and, though it rejected King Hussein's call for a Middle East peace settlement based on Resolution 242, left the door open for future contacts between Arafat and Hussein. Soon after, on 11 February 1985, the two leaders reached an agreement on joint Jordanian-Palestinian steps to be taken towards a Middle East settlement. The PNC's Amman session and the 11 February agreement, were received in Moscow with bitter disappointment and severe apprehensions. Having courted the 'conservative' Arab states for several months, the Chernenko regime felt that its Middle East campaign was running out of steam and that the USSR was yet again losing the political initiative to the United States. These fears were compounded by Arafat's moves, which revived old Soviet worries about a PLO shift towards the Reagan Plan.

In these circumstances, the USSR moved cautiously to improve the strained atmosphere between itself and Syria. While seeking to maintain the modest momentum in its relations with Jordan, the USSR, in deference to Syria, quietly gave up the idea of King Hussein's visit to Moscow, scheduled for late 1984.[40] In the light of the UN-sponsored Lebanese-Israeli talks, which began in early November on Israel's withdrawal from Lebanon, Moscow also resumed its vocal support for what it defined as 'Syria's legitimate interest in Lebanon'. 'In connection with the evident difficulties at the talks and the murkiness of their prospects, quite a lot is being said in the Israeli and US press about Syria and its alleged negative influence both on the overall situation in the region and on the nature of Israeli-Lebanese relations,' wrote Aleksander Bovin in

Izvestiya on 18 November 1984. 'However, the facts refute this assessment of the matter,' he stated:

There are historical, geographical, cultural and ethnic factors
... which determine Syria's interest in being bordered by a
stable and domestically settled state, which is part of the Arab
world and whose government is capable of taking Syria's interests and concerns into account ... Syria's special interest in
Lebanese affairs is recognized by the Arab world. It is no
accident that Syrian troops comprised the backbone of the
inter-Arab peacekeeping forces in Lebanon ... [Hence] only a
solution which is simultaneously based on Lebanon's sovereign
rights to all Lebanese territory and which takes into account
Syria's legitimate interests is possible.[41]

From late 1984 onwards, the USSR resumed its support for Syria
in its feud with the PLO leadership: deploring in strong terms the
Arafat-Hussein agreement of 11 February 1985 as leading to the
'destruction of the reputation of and respect for the PLO, and also
damaging its role as the sole legitimate representative of the
Palestinian people',[42] the Soviets urged Arafat and his followers to
mend the rift with Syria.

Gorbachev: continuity or change?
To judge by the announcement of a three-day public mourning in
Syria over the death of Konstantin Chernenko on 10 March 1985,
the ageing leader's attempts to remove the strains in Soviet- Syrian
relations had been fully successful. But if the Syrians had cherished
any expectations that the new Soviet Secretary-General, Mikhail
Gorbachev, would continue the consolidation of bilateral relations
to the peak reached under Andropov, they were quick to realize that
the forceful and resolute backing of their brinkmanship tactics
during Andropov's brief period of power was the exception rather
than the rule as far as Soviet-Syrian relations were concerned. Like
Brezhnev and Chernenko, Gorbachev preached caution and
restraint, emphasizing the political option as the means of solving
the Arab-Israeli conflict. Moreover, like his immediate predecessor,
the new leader sought to prevent the United States from monopoliz-
ing the re-emerging political process in the Arab-Israeli sphere: he
courted the conservative Arab states (e.g., establishing diplomatic

relations with Oman and the United Arab Emirates in 1985, rescheduling Egypt's military debts and signing new economic agreements with this country in 1987) and, perhaps more alarming from the Syrian point of view, laid great emphasis on the normalization of relations with Israel.

Soviet interest in Israel was, of course, no new development: Moscow's awareness of the damage done to its regional standing by the severance of diplomatic relations with Israel led it to maintain direct and indirect channels of communication with Israel, and even to make occasional conciliatory gestures towards that country. Yet the scope and intensity of the Soviet-Israeli interaction were considerably widened and enhanced after Gorbachev assumed office. In July 1985 the Soviet and Israeli ambassadors to France held a secret meeting in Paris in which they reportedly discussed issues such as the restoration of bilateral relations and the possibility of a Syrian-Israeli agreement on the Golan Heights.[43] A year later, in August 1986, foreign ministry officials from the two countries met in Helsinki to discuss consular matters. Though it ended on a slightly sour note, the Helsinki meeting was followed by bilateral contacts at a relatively high level,[44] and in July 1987 a Soviet consulate was set up in Israel, so far without reciprocation. In January-February 1988, when Israel was exercising strong measures to stem the mounting tide of Palestinian unrest in the West Bank, the Soviets reiterated their willingness to accept an Israeli consular delegation in Moscow and to re-establish diplomatic relations with Israel once a negotiations process on an Arab-Israeli settlement was under way within the framework of an international conference.[45] This pledge was reiterated in May 1988 by Gorbachev himself during his summit meeting with Reagan. In all these dealings with Israel, the Soviets apparently used their relationship with Syria as a trump card, implying that they had both the willingness and the capability to exercise influence over Damascus.[46]

Gorbachev also followed his predecessor in exploiting the growing internal and external plight of the Asad regime. On the domestic front, the economic crisis that had been overtaking Syria since the early 1980s grew rapidly in 1985–7: with its GDP in a steady decline from 1983 onwards and foreign-currency reserves dwindling to cover only a few weeks' imports, Syria found it increasingly difficult to earn more from exports or to get the necessary capital to finance its current-account deficit. The outcome was greater austerity measures and continued cutbacks in the Syrian ground forces from late 1986 onwards, with regular units being dismantled and their weaponry put in storage.[47] This combination led to a deterioration in Syria's internal security (e.g., a bombing campaign in Syrian towns, reported coup attempts in the autumn of 1986 and in the spring of 1987), as well as more active jockeying for position within the regime.[48]

Syria's external position was no more enviable. Having brought about the withdrawal of external forces from Lebanon (in the summer of 1985 Israel completed its pull-back from Lebanon, with the exception of limited forces left within a 'security zone' in the areas immediately adjoining Israeli territory), Asad discovered once again the problem of imposing law and order on this fractious country. A Syrian-engineered tripartite agreement, signed in Damascus on 28 December 1985 between the Shi'ite leader, Nabih Berri, the Druze leader, Walid Jumblatt, and the Maronite leader, Elie Hobeika, collapsed within a fortnight of its conclusion. In addition, Syria's authority in Lebanon was increasingly challenged throughout 1986 and 1987, both by the pro-Iranian extremist Shi'ite organization, the Hizbollah, and by Iran's mounting influence in Lebanese domestic affairs.

Friction between Syria and the Hizbollah unsettled Syria's relationship with its strategic ally, Iran. Also, although it improved its relations with Jordan after 1985, Syria's support for Iran in the Iran-Iraq War strained its relations with the conservative Arab countries, and by mid-1986 most of the Gulf states had stopped their financial aid to Syria, given hitherto in accordance with the 1978 Baghdad decisions.

To make matters worse, Syria's insecurity increased considerably following its second missile crisis with Israel in December 1985 – January 1986[49] and the crisis after the abortive attempt to blow up an Israeli El-Al plane in London in April 1986. Not only did the London incident put Damascus in direct confrontation with Great Britain (and, to a lesser extent, the United States), but it also appeared to bring Israel and Syria to the verge of armed conflict. Had the terrorist act been successful, Israel would most probably have felt compelled to respond with a significant military strike. As things stood – and notwithstanding vehement Syrian denials of any connection with the London incident, which neither the Israelis nor the British took seriously – Jerusalem wavered between the need for restraint and the urge to deter, if not punish, Syria; it therefore sent out equivocal signals, combining threats of retaliation with reassurances that Israel harboured no aggressive designs against Damascus. Syria reacted to these contradictory signals by building up its forces on the Golan Heights and in the Beq'a, as well as by unleashing a strident propaganda campaign highlighting its steadfastness in the face of the 'Israeli threat'. So tense was the situation along the Syrian-Israeli border that in mid-May the American administration took care to warn the two countries, both covertly and overtly, against going to war.

Though limited to the diplomatic sphere, London's reaction was no less harsh than that of Israel: on 10 May the British authorities expelled three Syrian diplomats for complicity in the incident, after Syria rejected a request that their diplomatic immunity be waived so that they could be questioned about the El-Al bombing attempt; some five months later, on 24 October 1986, Britain took the extreme step of breaking off diplomatic relations with Syria, after a London court found Syrian involvement in the April incident. The United States and Canada followed suit in a gesture of solidarity, and by 10 November Britain had convinced its EC counterparts, except Greece, to impose limited sanctions on Syria.

The American administration, having launched a massive air raid on the Libyan cities of Tripoli and Benghazi on 15 April in retaliation for alleged Libyan complicity in terrorist activities, did not fail to caution Syria: on 24 April Reagan announced that he would not rule out military retaliation against Syria (and Iran) if they could be linked to terrorist acts. And the same theme was reiterated a day later by George Shultz, who, while denying the existence of concrete plans for an attack on Syria (and Iran), emphasized his country's determination to employ force against countries connected with terrorism.[50]

With its main Middle Eastern ally beset by domestic problems and facing a concerted diplomatic onslaught by the West, as well as the risk of military confrontation with Israel, Moscow felt able to pursue a regional policy with no reference to Damascus's wishes, and to put pressure on Syria in an attempt to bring it into line with Soviet objectives. Accordingly, Gorbachev made clear to Asad both his reluctance to support Syria's goal of 'strategic parity' with Israel and his dissatisfaction with the continuing Syrian-Palestinian and Syrian-Iraqi rifts. This position was apparently clarified to Asad during his first meeting with Mikhail Gorbachev in June 1985, when he failed to obtain a Soviet agreement to support Syria's military needs.[51] It was further underlined by the Soviet behaviour during the second missile and El-Al bombing crises. On both occasions the USSR found itself in the awkward position of having to choose between its desire to appear as the staunch supporter of the Arab cause and its fear of escalation; between its anxiety to deny the West, in particular the United States, any gains, and its reluctance to risk a superpower confrontation. The outcome was the tried combination of vocal endorsement of the Syrian stand, on the one hand, and avoidance of clear and unequivocal commitment to Syria, on the other.

Thus, while justifying the deployment of surface-to-air missiles along the Syrian border on grounds of 'self-defence and the protection of Syria's ally, sovereign Lebanon' and describing the Israeli (and American) demand for the withdrawal of the missiles as an 'impudent interference in Syria's internal affairs [reflecting] the imperial aspirations of Washington and Tel Aviv',[52] Moscow took care not to give any indication of readiness to support Damascus militarily should the crisis escalate into an open conflagration. The Soviet media did not mention the introduction of Syrian missiles into Lebanon, stating that the deployment of missiles took place within Syria's national borders.[53] It is possible that this omission meant to serve as both an implicit criticism of Syria's decision to challenge Israel in Lebanon and a delineation of the geographical limits of Soviet support for Syria.

More significant, the Soviets avoided any allusion to the Friendship and Cooperation Treaty. The only reference to the treaty throughout the crisis came in the form of an interview given to the Kuwaiti newspaper *Al Watan* on 29 December 1985 by the Deputy Chief of the International Department of the CPSU Central Committee, Karen Brutents, who was at the time on a visit to Kuwait: 'I would like to remind you that we stand by Syria, with whom we have a treaty of cooperation, and we observe the spirit and the text of the treaty. Thus Syria will not be alone in face of any Israeli aggression.' Yet, as a salient exception to the otherwise extremely cautious tone of Soviet references to the crisis, Brutents's pledge of support only served to highlight the ambiguity of Moscow's commitment to Syrian security. During the crisis following the El-Al incident not only did the Soviet media refrain from any mention of the Friendship and Cooperation Treaty, but they also took care to stress that Syria had no real need of Soviet military support: 'Syria, as its leaders have said, has enough power to defend its sovereignty and independence.'[54]

Even the most notable manifestation of Soviet support for Damascus during the second crisis – namely, Vice-President Khaddam's working visit to Moscow on 27–29 May 1986 – revealed the USSR's dilemma. Although Gorbachev warned that any strike against Syria would entail 'incalculable consequences',[55] and although an agreement on increased arms supplies, including the delivery of MiG-29 aircraft, was signed,[56] the Soviets put pressure on Syria to avoid escalation. They emphasized to Khaddam the futility of a resort to force and the need for 'political settlement of regional conflicts through collective efforts'.[57] They also clarified that the backing of Syria was not an exclusively Soviet, but primarily an all-Arab, responsibility. As the Soviet President, Andrei Gromyko, said in his dinner speech honouring Khaddam: 'In the USSR there is the conviction that if the Arabs succeed in ensuring unity in their ranks, it would be an effective weapon resisting their enemies' intrigues.'[58] Gorbachev is also said to have pointed out to Khaddam that, owing to the USSR's logistical and operational constraints, the burden of containing any 'lightning attack' on Syria would lie on Damascus's shoulders alone.[59] Finally, the Soviets raised once again the issues clouding Soviet-Syrian relations: namely, the Asad-Arafat rift and Syria's support for Iran. This last issue was particularly urgent at that time given Iran's series of military successes, which, however limited, rekindled international fears of an Iranian victory in the Gulf War.[60]

Interestingly enough, neither Gorbachev's less forthcoming attitude towards Syria nor his attempts to court both the 'conservative' Arab regimes and Israel led to serious strains in Soviet-Syrian relations. On the contrary, throughout 1986 and 1987 Syria sought to highlight its cordial relations with the USSR and, moreover, took two important steps that complied with Moscow's wishes: namely, the *rapprochement* with Jordan, and the intensification of its pronounced support for an international conference.

On 29 December 1985, after a series of preparatory contacts, King Hussein arrived in Damascus for his first visit in a decade, and in early 1986 he and Asad exchanged visits. The reconciliation, which resulted from both Jordanian disappointment with Yasser Arafat's tactics of procrastination and Hussein's awareness that any progress towards a settlement would require at least tacit Syrian approval, soon produced results: on 19 February 1986 Hussein announced his decision to end Jordan's partnership with the PLO, and during that summer he closed down all of the 25 Al-Fath offices that had been allowed to open in Jordan after the November 1984 Palestinian National Council in Amman.

The Syrian-Jordanian *rapprochement* was received by Moscow with considerable satisfaction.[61] First, Hussein's move against the PLO forestalled Arafat's gradual shift towards an American-inspired solution based on the Reagan Plan, and paved the way for the PLO to return to a more 'progressive' approach. This was eventually achieved at the 18th session of the Palestinian National Council in Algiers in April 1987, when Arafat dissociated himself completely from the February 1985 agreement with Hussein. Second, the growing Syrian-Jordanian cooperation might contain the seeds of a *rapprochement* between Syria and Iraq – something Hussein had worked hard to achieve. Despite the long-standing enmity between the Syrian and Iraqi leaderships (in 1986 Syria exploited King Hussein's attempts at mediation in order to manoeuvre Iran into augmenting its aid to Syria), some progress, albeit modest, was made in this direction, culminating in a meeting between Asad and the Iraqi leader, Saddam Hussein, during the Amman Arab summit of November 1987.

Finally, having dropped the PLO from his peace efforts, Hussein joined Syria in propagating the idea of an international conference on the Middle East. While Hussein's perception of an international conference differed from that of the Soviet Union, the resurrection of the idea of such a conference among practically all the Arab states bordering Israel (Egypt included) was certainly a positive development from the Soviet point of view. Indeed, Syria's main contribution to Soviet Middle Eastern policy at the time was its strong support for the proposed conference.[62]

These developments, together with Syria's continued weakness, reduced Soviet apprehensions of a Syrian-inspired escalation and encouraged Moscow to respond to Damascus's military and economic needs. Thus, in contrast with Asad's 1985 Moscow visit, the second meeting between Asad and Gorbachev, on 23–25 April 1987, bore concrete and positive fruit from the Syrian point of view. First, it produced a series of bilateral agreements on technical and economic cooperation, including the development of Syria's phosphate and oil industries, and the construction of the hydro-electric Tishrin Dam on the Euphrates. Second, Moscow agreed to reschedule Syria's $15 billion debt and to conclude a new arms deal, which apparently included the coveted MiG-29 aircraft, promised to Khaddam a year earlier but withheld from Syria until then;[63] within a couple of months of the visit, Syria received its first delivery of MiG-29s.[64] Finally, the two parties reconfirmed their full resolve 'to continue strengthening their mutual trust, links at many levels and close relations which . . . are in the national interests of the Soviet and Syrian peoples'.[65]

That this statement reflected a real Soviet intention to warm up bilateral relations was shown by the flood of Soviet delegations to Damascus during the months following Asad's visit: in June 1987 alone Damascus hosted no fewer than five official Soviet guests. In addition, on 22 July 1987 a Syrian cosmonaut took off in the Soviet spaceship *Soyuz TM-3*; this event received much publicity in both countries and was characterized by Mikhail Gorbachev as 'a striking page in the annals of the development and strengthening of Soviet-Syrian friendship'.[66]

However, Gorbachev made Asad aware of the strings attached to Moscow's support for Syria, emphasizing that 'the reliance on military force in settling the Arab-Israeli conflict has completely lost its credibility'.[67] While this statement was partly directed towards Israel, and even though the belief itself had been preached by the Soviets to their Arab allies from the early 1970s onwards, the futility of reliance on military force was stressed by Gorbachev 'with more conviction and vigour than ever before'.[68] This view was supported by a joint communiqué on the importance of reconvening an international conference, by Gorbachev's reference to the abnormality of the absence of Soviet-Israeli diplomatic relations,[69] and by the outspoken Soviet criticism of the concept of 'strategic parity' in the wake of Asad's visit. 'In our view,' argued *Izvestiya*'s Middle Eastern commentator, Konstantin Geyvendov, in an interview with the Kuwaiti newspaper *Al-Anba* on 12 September 1987, 'the talk about strategic parity aims at diverting attention from the question of achieving security and peace in the Middle East . . . [It just] does not have any meaning.'

Nor did Gorbachev fail to mention Syria's relations with the PLO and Iraq. During his dinner speech in honour of Asad he pronounced his satisfaction with the proceedings of the PNC's Algiers session, which took place at the same time as Asad's visit. Similarly, he expressed deep concern at the continuation of the Iran-Iraq War, emphasizing the 'unchanging position of the Soviet Union' regarding the conflict.[70] The Syrian position on these two issues was, naturally, more equivocal. On the one hand, Asad could draw a measure of comfort from Arafat's dissociation of himself from the February 1985 agreement: this had been a long-standing Syrian objective. But as the agreement was already an empty document, having been abrogated by King Hussein a year earlier, he viewed the move as an undesirable tactical development which rallied the PLO behind Arafat, thereby rendering the subservience of the PLO to Syrian wishes an unlikely eventuality. Indeed, his fears seemed to be confirmed by the participation of two of Syria's supporters, George Habash and Naif Hawatma, at the PNC's session – against Damascus's wish and largely as a result of Soviet efforts.

Yet neither of these issues was allowed by Asad to lead to a confrontation with the Soviets. Hence, the joint communiqué contained the Soviet formula that 'the need to restore unity in the ranks of the Palestinian resistance movement on a principled, anti-imperialist platform was stressed'.[71] Regarding the Iran-Iraq conflict, Asad consented to a meeting with Saddam Hussein, which took place in Jordan immediately upon Asad's return from Moscow.[72] Neither this meeting nor the meeting with Saddam Hussein during the Amman summit reflected a fundamental change in Syria's attitude towards its perennial rival. Yet they provide another indication, however limited, of the improved Soviet position *vis-à-vis* Syria, which can be traced back to 1977.

7
CONCLUSIONS

Dating back to November 1970, Soviet relations with the Asad regime form the most enduring and uninterrupted tie that the USSR has maintained with any Middle Eastern leader in the postwar era. During this period Syria has developed into Moscow's most prominent ally in the Middle East. Soviet military support for Syria during the first half of the 1980s was worth around $8 billion and exceeded that rendered to any other Middle Eastern country or, indeed, Latin America, East Asia or sub-Saharan Africa.[1] The Soviet relationship with Asad's Syria offers an illuminating insight into both the dynamics of a great-power/small-state relationship, with its inherent constraints and opportunities for both parties, and the scope and intensity of Soviet interests in the Middle East.

A marriage of convenience
Analyses of international politics, especially great-power/small-state relationships, often fall within one of the following two broad categories: the *patron-client relationship* and the *tail wags the dog* (or, *the power of the weak*). The first mode of analysis argues that relationships between actors of unequal power and status favour, by and large, the patron, whose bargaining position is by definition better than that of the client (even taking into account the element of reciprocity in the relationship). Ranging from a more or less symbiotic partnership to a situation of unilateral exploitation, patron – client relations are based on reciprocity in the exchange of

material goods or protection for services, loyalty and deference to the patron:

> The weak state can still get protection or material aid in time of need, but in return it has to render services which considerably limit its freedom of action and decision on a large variety of international issues. On almost every issue it has to follow the great power's lead and continuously try to please it. Sometimes the weak state is asked to do so; sometimes, on its own initiative, it tries to guess what the great power would like it to do ... [The] client state makes decisions regarding its foreign policy with one ear to the wishes of the great power ... In the ideal form of patron – client relations, the client state voluntarily sets its own limits on action and makes decisions in support of the great power, hoping by such acts either to get immediate positive rewards from the great power or to accumulate goodwill and credit for the future.[2]

The tail wags the dog paradigm, on the other hand, starts from the assumption that the structural traits of the contemporary international system, particularly the inter-bloc polarization and the consequent superpower competition for allies, together with the advent of nuclear weaponry on the international scene, have significantly improved the bargaining power of small actors *vis-à-vis* the great powers:

> The factors that inhibit the superpowers' exploitation of their enormous military machines for other purposes *ipso facto* increase the lesser states' capacity to use their own power for denial against the superpowers and their allies. When the eagle's claws are clipped the dove can save its life ... The smaller states, feeling stronger in their defences against threats from the superpowers, are often able and willing to pursue goals beyond mere survival and security. Conversely, the superpowers, encumbered by their nuclear power, must concentrate as never before on the requirements of security and survival.[3]

These two diametrically opposed paradigms have been applied to the analysis of Soviet-Arab relations in general, and the Soviet-Syrian relationship in particular. 'The terms of the Soviet-Syrian relationship are typical of ... patron-client relationships' is one view: 'The Soviets provide Syria with assistance necessary for it to be effective in regional policy, and in exchange the Soviets obtain a presence in Syria as well as Syrian support for Soviet actions in areas outside Syria's core interest.'[4] And the distance from this view to the belief that Syria is merely a Soviet proxy, 'the Cuba of the Middle East', is short:

> Syrian leaders consistently and closely identify with Soviet goals ... [Syria] has concurred with the USSR on every significant issue in the General Assembly in recent years ... The USSR derives many benefits from its close relations with Damascus. In particular, Syria provides an eastern Mediterranean base, an air-defence link, and an agency for terrorism ... In return, Syria's cause receives support from the whole Soviet bloc.[5]

Such views contrast with analyses emphasizing the abundant leverage given to Middle Eastern countries in their relations with the Soviet Union: 'The Soviets, much like their American rivals, and perhaps even more so, do not control their Middle Eastern allies. They are constrained by their global interests to such an extent that they have little choice but to play to the tune of their far weaker allies.'[6]

However intriguing, both approaches are equally misconceived. Just as Syria cannot be considered a Soviet client, 'voluntarily setting its own limits on action and making decisions regarding its foreign policy with one ear to the wishes of the great power', so the USSR cannot be labelled a passive, reactive actor, 'playing to the tune of its weaker allies'. If anything, the Soviet-Syrian relationship should be portrayed in terms of a mutually beneficial *strategic interdependence* between two allies: a relationship favouring each partner in accordance with the vicissitudes in regional and global affairs.

The Middle East, perhaps more than any other subsystem in today's world, embodies the structural constraints imposed by the international system on the manoeuvrability of the great powers; the Soviet-Syrian relationship is therefore *a priori* tilted in Damascus's favour. A highly strategic area for the two great-power blocs, given both its proximity to the USSR's southern borders and its huge oil deposits, this region has been an attractive target for imperialism.

While this jeopardized the independent development of local actors before World War II, great-power rivalry in the Middle East in the postwar era, with both blocs seeking to enlist as many local allies as possible, has significantly improved the bargaining position of the regional states. Thus, by remaining Moscow's only ally in the Arab-Israeli sphere after October 1973 and by being the sole channel through which the USSR has been able to resist the monopolization of the political process by the United States, Syria enjoys real leverage over its more powerful ally.

Fortunately for Moscow, this imbalance has gradually disappeared since 1977, following the evolution of a separate Egyptian-Israeli peace process, on the one hand, and the mounting domestic opposition to the Asad regime, on the other. Faced with these challenges, Syria's sense of vulnerability rose sharply, driving it to opt for a more concrete Soviet political and military commitment. This restored balance to the relationship.

The delicate interplay between Damascus's structural preponderance and Moscow's circumstantial advantage forms the basis for the present Soviet Syrian partnership. Both countries have reaped significant, albeit not always symmetrical, political, economic and strategic gains from the relationship. Asad's Syria has been *the* Middle Eastern ally for the Soviet Union since the mid-1970s, promoting the fundamental goal of eradicating Western influence in this crucial region on the southern borders of the USSR, and offering the USSR an important, if limited, military foothold. Moscow, meanwhile, has been Syria's main strategic ally: it has supplied political, economic and strategic aid, and been both a counterbalance to American intervention in the area and a deterrent (however minor) to Israel's 'aggressive designs'. Soviet military backing and political support is largely responsible for Syria's success in asserting itself as a leading regional power whose presence cannot be ignored. And it is mainly thanks to Syria that the USSR has not been pushed to the sidelines of the Arab-Israeli conflict.

The military sphere has been the most important in Soviet-Syrian relations. It is here that the Soviets have made their heaviest investments and have reaped the most tangible gains (e.g., naval facilities in Syrian ports and hard currency earnings). In doing so they have relied on two parallel courses of action: military involvement (arms supplies and advisory support) and military intervention (assistance rendered by regular Soviet units). Since the former provides a more subtle means of backing that does not necessitate direct Soviet engagement in the military and strategic affairs of the particular region, it has been the most common means of Soviet military support for Syria in both peace- and wartime. Over the past two decades of the Asad regime the Soviets have decisively contributed, through aid and advice, to the transformation of the Syrian armed forces into one of the leading military powers in the Middle East. This process has led, in turn, to the expansion of the Soviet advisory presence in Syria from 1,000 in 1970 to nearly 3,000 in the mid-1980s.

In contrast with their generous military involvement in Syria, the Soviets have been very careful to limit intervention to the lowest possible level. Thus, apart from times of war when circumstances have compelled Moscow to commit regular units to demonstrative, or even fighting, activities on behalf of Syria (e.g., the Mediterranean Squadron, dispatch of air-defence units, alert of airborne brigades), the independent Soviet presence in Syria has been very limited in comparison with, for example, the Soviet presence in Egypt in the early 1970s. Though it was partly dictated by Asad's reluctance to compromise Syrian sovereignty, the limited Soviet peacetime presence was also motivated by Moscow's awareness of the potentially adverse implications of intervention. Indeed, having obtained access to port facilities in Tartus in 1976, the Soviets never sought to expand their naval presence beyond catering for the minimum supportive requirements of their Mediterranean Squadron. No wonder therefore that the Soviet air-defence units that appeared in Syria during the October War and after the 1982 Lebanon War were quickly and quietly withdrawn after they had handed over control to the Syrians.

The political realm has been the most elusive and fluctuating dimension of the Soviet-Syrian relationship. Close cooperation, convergence and amity have suddenly turned to confrontation, alienation and even enmity. Yet occasional disagreements, frictions and manipulations apart, neither party has compromised core interests for the sake of the partnership. With the passage of time, the two allies have developed finely tuned 'synchronization mechanisms' for each other's sensitivities and goals; these enable them to recognize the limits of influence, on the one hand, and to exploit the fields of effective cooperation, on the other. The USSR has learnt to live with Syria's rejection of Israel's right to exist, its deep enmity for the Iraqi Ba'th regime and its overriding interest in Lebanon, while Syria has acquiesced in Moscow's emphasis on Israel's right to a secure existence, its continued support for Iraq and its reluctance to accept the Syrian interpretation of the military obligations embodied in the Friendship and Cooperation Treaty.

The vicissitudes in the political sphere have been partially balanced by economic factors which, though playing a subordinate role, have injected a measure of stability into Soviet-Syrian relations. With the exception of a few years when Syria enjoyed the economic prosperity of rising oil prices and generous Arab support, the economic gains reaped for the Soviet Union from its various forms of aid to Syria have been limited. Rather, economic aid has served to underline Soviet goodwill towards Syria, so as to promote the USSR's political goals there. Soviet economic aid has been extensive, providing for the development of the Syrian infrastructure in the fields of agriculture (growing of cotton, farm mechanization), irrigation (erection of dams), transportation (railway system, ports) and industry, where the USSR has helped to establish Syria's oil industry by increasing the state's oil storage capacity and assisting Syria in setting up its national drilling company.

For the USSR, the highly personalized nature of Arab politics has been a mixed blessing. In dealing with a political system that tends to 'elevate the leader, particularly in radical states, to a position of dominance over state institutions',[7] the Soviets have often found their regional investments dependent on the views and idiosyncrasies of specific leaders. Just as Abd Al-Nasser's radical zeal provided the avenue along which the Soviets made their way into Egypt, so Moscow's failure to come to terms with Nasser's successor led to the loss of its most prominent Middle Eastern ally. Similarly, it was Moscow's success in striking the right balance between Hafiz Asad's ambitious world-view and Soviet Middle Eastern interests which accounts for the continuity of the close Soviet-Syrian relationship.

Moscow was, however, aided by the remarkable consistency of Asad's goals, despite the tactical pragmatism of the Syrian leader. The most important of the traditional articles of belief underlying Syria's external behaviour, to which he remained committed, was the idea of 'Greater Syria'. This, together with the conviction that 'Syria is the geopolitical heart of the region' and the 'maker of peace and war' in the Middle East,[8] as well as the belief that 'Syria alone stands in the way of the Israeli attempt to establish the "Torah

State" from the Euphrates to the Nile',[9] constitutes Asad's
perceptual framework: a unique mixture of grand aspirations,
missionary zeal and perennial insecurity. This world-view has, in
turn, made alliance with the Soviet Union a strategic necessity. In
the Syrian view:

> The relations with the Soviet Union are far deeper than some
> people are trying to portray. The Soviet Union is neither a
> depot or shop for the sale of arms nor a card to be played in
> the market of international politics. For Syria, relations are of
> strategic importance and are indispensable from a national
> standpoint, to which there is no alternative for Syria or the
> Arabs in the present international conditions.[10]

Asad's world-view has not always been in harmony with
Moscow's regional aims, as the overriding concern of Soviet policy
towards Syria from Brezhnev to Gorbachev (with the qualified
exception of Andropov's brief period of power, when the tide of
events forced the USSR to be more supportive of the Syrian
position) has been the attainment and preservation of stability. In
the sphere of the Arab-Israeli conflict, as in the realm of inter-Arab
politics, the Soviets have preached restraint and moderation to
Syria, emphasizing the advantages of a negotiated settlement over
the military option. Thus, in almost every visit paid by Asad to the
USSR – even at times when the USSR has been in a weak position
vis-à-vis Syria (e.g., the April 1974 and 1977 visits) – the Soviets
made clear their disapproval of Syria's rejection of the legitimacy of
Israel[11] by emphasizing the latter's right to a secure existence. This
disapproval found its most salient expression when Gorbachev
openly discredited the military option during and after the April
1987 visit. Moreover, whenever the Soviets have deemed Syria's
actions to endanger regional stability, they have applied pressure on
Damascus and shown their dissatisfaction with Syrian behaviour, at
the risk of damaging Soviet-Syrian relations.

True, having failed to moderate Syria's course, the Soviets have
found themselves more than once compelled to lend full support to
Syria; yet the abundant Soviet crisis and wartime aid was essentially
reactive, circumspect and incremental, reflecting the Soviet leadership's interest in containing conflict. Thus, in all Syrian-Israeli
armed confrontations the USSR has been very careful to avoid any
commitment of regular units until its more 'conventional' modes of

support (namely, arms shipments and advisory assistance) have failed to achieve their goals. Accordingly, Soviet military intervention – with the partial exception of the naval sphere – has never taken place before Syria has faced a severe operational predicament. Moreover, even the commitment of naval forces has been carried out in a circumspect manner, designed to help the Syrian forces cut their losses, and to hold back or deter the opposing forces, rather than to move them to the offensive.

Implications for the West
What are the implications of this state of affairs for the West? Given Asad's uncompromising views on the Arab-Israeli conflict and his consequent belief that the Soviet-Syrian relationship is a vital strategic bond, a dramatic reversal of Syria's global orientation, Egypt-style, seems rather unlikely (though not completely inconceivable), at least as long as Asad stays in power.

This by no means makes Syria a 'lost cause' for the West. Asad has been careful (though not always sufficiently) not to burn his boats with the Western powers. West European trade still figures prominently in Syria's overall trade, while the occasional warming-up of political and military relations (e.g., Asad's 1976 visit to France and Mitterrand's 1984 visit to Damascus) has been employed by Syria to extract concessions from the USSR. In this context, however, a distinction should be made between Syria's attitude towards Western Europe and towards the United States. While maintaining much wider economic relations with Western Europe, and viewing this region in far less negative terms than the United States, Asad is fully aware that it is Washington, and not the European capitals, which can exert leverage over Israel; indeed, such a leverage becomes all the more important in the light of Syria's growing economic problems, which constrain its ability to pursue ambitious military expansion.

Syria views Western Europe, therefore, in largely instrumental terms: namely, as a highly useful trade partner and an intermediary stage on Syria's road to Washington. This, in turn, means that Syrian-European political relations are less susceptible to sudden changes than Syrian-American relations, though the potential for their development is more limited. Moreover, one should not pin too high a hope on America's ability to establish a substantive and enduring influence over Syria. First, given the structural constraints on great-power conduct in the Middle East, exploited to the full by Syria in its relations with Moscow, it is questionable whether Syria would be more responsive to American interests than it has been to Soviet. Second, since the USA's ability to deliver Syria's minimum political demand, the Golan Heights, remains limited, there is practically nothing that Washington could offer Damascus beyond what the Soviets have already delivered.

As far as the USSR is concerned, Soviet-Syrian relations should provide a major operational lesson for the West, in particular the United States. Since the Soviet Union, having inescapable Middle Eastern interests, cannot and will not distance itself from the affairs of this region, the only certain way to reduce its interference in the Middle East is to solve the Arab-Israeli conflict, which is the lodestone for Western intervention and, in consequence, the major threat to Soviet interests. Yet as the USSR can never accept a *Pax Americana*, which would leave its backyard under hostile external control, the United States should strive to bring the USSR back into the mainstream of Arab-Israeli diplomacy. Although such a move might antagonize some regional allies, it would best serve Western interests by making possible a stable settlement.

The question should now be raised, whether and to what extent the USSR can be considered a reliable partner in a Middle Eastern peace settlement. Here the record of Soviet-Syrian relations beomes most illuminating, for during the past two decades the Soviets have gone to great lengths to persuade Syria to choose the political over the military option, even at the risk of confrontation with this extremely important ally. These efforts have ranged from the Soviet success in May 1973 in persuading Asad to postpone the planned war so as to give diplomacy a chance, to the less successful attempts, in 1973–4, to bring Syria to the Geneva conference, to Gorbachev's frank words with Asad during the April 1987 visit. They include attempts to twist Syria's arm by reducing arms supplies and by courting Israel and the conservative Arab states.

More than anything, this policy reflects a clear recognition that the Arab-Israeli conflict has long outlived its usefulness to Soviet Middle Eastern interests. True, the conflict initially enabled the USSR to entrench its presence in the region, but this presence has never been an end in itself, rather a means to promote Soviet security by eliminating external intervention in the Middle East and cultivating a favourable local environment. This goal can best be achieved by neutralizing potential sources of instability, the most volatile of which is the Arab-Israeli conflict. Moreover, the Gorbachev years have witnessed a growing and more outspoken Soviet willingness to recognize the legitimacy of American interests in the Middle East; this, in turn, may form a better basis for superpower collaboration. As Mikhail Gorbachev wrote in his book *Perestroika*:

> We understand that under the present circumstances it is diffi-
> cult to reconcile the interests of the conflicting sides ...
> However, we do not at all want the process of working towards
> a settlement, or the very goals of this process, in some way to
> infringe upon the interests of the United States and the West.
> We are not bent on elbowing the United States out of the
> Middle East – this is simply unrealistic. But the United States
> should not commit itself to unrealistic goals either. The main
> thing here is to take the interests of all sides into considera-
> tion.[12]

NOTES

Chapter 1

1 The term Middle East as employed in this study encompasses the area referred to by the Soviets as the Near East (*Blizhni Vostok*) and Middle East (*Srednii Vostok*): namely, Turkey, Iran, Afghanistan, Iraq, the countries of the Arabian Peninsula, Jordan, Syria, Israel, Lebanon, Egypt.

2 Royal Institute of International Affairs, *Documents on International Affairs, 1955* (London: Oxford University Press, 1958), p. 303.

3 The only other Third World area in close proximity to the USSR is Southeast Asia; however, unlike the Middle East, this area is not directly contiguous to the Soviet border, but separated from it by China.

4 Y. Primakov, *Anatomy of the Middle East Conflict* (Moscow: Nauka, 1979), p. 145.

5 P. Seale, *The Struggle for Syria* (London: Oxford University Press for the RIIA, 1965), p. 234.

6 *Ibid.* According to Seale, it was Syria rather than Egypt that broke the Western monopoly of arms supplies to the Middle East by signing in 1954 a small arms deal with Czechoslovakia.

7 For a description of Soviet support for Syria during the 1957 crisis see, for example, W.Z. Laqueur, *The Soviet Union and the Middle East* (London: Routledge & Kegan Paul, 1959), pp. 247–64; Seale, *The Struggle for Syria*, pp. 289–302; J.M. McConnell, 'Doctrine and Capabilities', in B. Dismukes and J.McConnell (eds.), *Soviet Naval Diplomacy* (New York: Pergamon, 1979), pp. 7–10.

8 G. Lenczowski, *Soviet Advances in the Middle East* (Washington: American Enterprise Institute, 1971), p. 114.

9 *Guardian*, 19 June 1969.

10 *Al-Nida(Beirut)*, *22 March 1969; L'Humanité* (Paris), 7 March 1969.

Chapter 2

1 *Damascus Domestic Service*, 16 November 1970.

2 For Soviet and Syrian descriptions of Asad's visit see: *Tass*, 3 February 1971; *Moscow Domestic Service in Russian*, 1, 3 February 1971; *Moscow in Arabic*, 31 January, 2, 3 February 1971; *Izvestiya*, 30 January 1971; *Damascus Domestic Service*, 3 February 1971. For Western accounts see: *The Times*, 2, 4 February 1971; *International Herald Tribune*, 5 February 1971; *New York Times*, 2 February 1971; *The Financial Times*, 2 February 1971.

3 *Tass*, 26 February 1972 (economic agreement); *Tass*, 13 May 1972; *Krasnaya Zvezda*, 16 May 1972; *Pravda*, 15 May 1972; *The Financial Times*, 15 May 1972; *New York Times*, 15 May 1972; *Guardian*, 11 May 1972 (Grechko's visit); G. Golan, *Yom Kippur and After* (Cambridge: Cambridge University Press, 1979), p.29 (Asad's deal); *International Herald Tribune*, 11 December 1972; *Daily Telegraph*, 7 December 1972 (Tlas's deal).

4 See Chapter 4, pp. 66–7.

5 On Moscow's opposition to the outbreak of war in the Middle East and its attempts to prevent it see E. Karsh 'Moscow and the Yom Kippur War: A Reappraisal', *Soviet Jewish Affairs*, Vol. 16, No. 1 (1986), pp. 3–19; also G. Golan, *Yom Kippur and After*, Chapter 2, and K. Dawisha, *Soviet Foreign Policy towards Egypt* (London: Macmillan, 1979), pp 65–6.

6 According to President Sadat, he did not inform Asad of his plan to go to war until the spring of 1973. This version was confirmed by President Asad some years later. See his interview with *Al-Sabah* (Amman), 10 June 1976.

7 It has become commonplace among Western analysts to view July 1972 as the major turning-point in Soviet-Syrian relations. See, for example, G. Golan, 'Syria and the Soviet Union since the Yom Kippur War', *Orbis*, Winter 1978, p. 777; M. Ma'oz, *Syria Under Hafiz Al-Asad: New Domestic and Foreign Policies* (Jerusalem: The Hebrew University, 1975), p. 22. Such views, nevertheless, are too sweeping. While there is little doubt that the summer 1972 events enhanced Syria's significance in Soviet eyes, they did not inject a novel element into Soviet-Syrian relations but rather served to reinforce existing trends, which had started after Asad's first visit to Moscow in February 1971. The extent of the Soviet tilt towards Syria at the time

should not be overemphasized: the Egyptian setback damaged Soviet strategic interests less than was initially assumed, since the USSR was allowed to maintain its naval facilities in Egypt.

8 *Newsweek*, 7 August 1972.
9 Y. Ben-Porat, 'The Yom Kippur War: A Mistake in May and a Surprise in October', *Ma'arachot*, No. 299 (July-August 1985), pp. 2, 6 (Hebrew). This article draws on classified information, not released before.
10 H. Kissinger, *Years of Upheaval*, (London: Weidenfeld & Nicolson, 1982), p. 461 (emphasis added).
11 M. Ma'oz, *Syria Under Hafiz Al-Asad*, p. 24.
12 For an Egyptian account of this incident see: H. Heikal, *The Road to Ramadan* (London: Collins, 1976), pp. 207-9, 212-14; Sadat's interviews with the *Observer* (19 March 1978) and with the Lebanese newspapers *Al-Nahar* (1 March 1974) and *Al-Anwar* (28 March 1974). Vinogradov's version was published in the Beirut daily *Al-Safir* on 17 April 1974. Sadat's account was confirmed several years later by the Syrian Foreign Minister, Abd Al-Khalim Khaddam. See *Tishrin*, 17 May 1980.
13 Indeed, Asad criticized the USSR, albeit indirectly, in the speech explaining his decision to accept Resolution 338 (*Damascus Domestic Service*, 29 October 1973).
14 *Ibid.*; Asad's interview with the West German journal *General Anzeiger*, brought by *L' Action* (Tunis), 8 May 1974.
15 S.S. Roberts, 'The October 1973 Arab-Israeli War', in B.Dismukes and J. McConnell (eds.), *Soviet Naval Diplomacy*, p. 208.
16 P. Jabber and R. Kolkowicz, 'The Arab-Israeli Wars of 1967 and 1973', in S. Kaplan (ed.), *Diplomacy of Power* (Washington: Brookings, 1981), p. 449.
17 B. Porter, *The USSR in Third World Conflicts* (New York: Cambridge University Press, 1984), p. 134.
18 J. Glassman, *Arms for the Arabs* (Baltimore: Johns Hopkins University Press, 1975), p. 134.
19 Roberts, 'The October 1973 Arab-Israeli War', pp. 196, 201.
20 B. Kalb and M. Kalb, *Kissinger* (Boston: Little, Brown, 1974), p. 470.
21 C. Herzog, *The War of Atonement* (Boston: Little, Brown, 1975), p. 136.
22 Insight Team of the London Sunday Times, *The Yom Kippur War* (Garden City, N.Y.: Doubleday, 1974), p. 409.
23 Herzog, *The War of Atonement*, p. 136.
24 See, for example, G. Mirskiy, 'The Middle East – New Factors', *New Times*, No. 48, 1973, pp. 18-19; Ye. Primakov, ' "Sbalansirovannyi Kurs" na Blizhnem Vostoke ili staraia politika inymi stredstvami?',

Mirovaya Ekonomika i Mezhdunarodnoe Otnosheniia, No. 12 (1976), pp. 46–50.

25 *Tass*, 18 December 1973; *Moscow in Arabic*, 25 December 1973. It should be noted that Syria's decision not to participate in the Geneva conference did not escape some Soviet criticism, however mild and indirect. See, for example, *Moscow in Arabic*, 20 December 1973.

26 See, for example, *Le Monde*, 27 December 1973; *Jerusalem Post*, 3, 14 February 1974.

27 *Deutsche Presse Agentur(DPA)* (Hamburg), 6 March 1974; *Daily Telegraph*, 6 March.

28 *Moscow Domestic Service in Russian*, 7 March 1974; *Damascus Domestic Service*, 7 March 1974 (emphasis added).

29 *Tass*, 13 April 1974.

30 *Iraqi News Agency(INA)* (Baghdad), 26 May 1974.

31 *International Herald Tribune*, 9 August 1974; *Daily Telegraph*, 8 July, 5 September 1974; *Guardian*, 29 April, 18 December 1974.

32 For the text of the communiqué, see *Pravda*, 30 May 1974; *Syrian Arab News Agency (SANA)* (Damascus), 29 May 1974.

33 See, for example, *Pravda*, 3, 4, 5 May 1974; *Moscow in Arabic*, 4, 5 May 1974; *Tass*, 3 May 1974.

34 *Moscow Domestic Service in Russian*, 30 May 1974.

35 See, for example, Asad's interview with *Al-Ahram* (Cairo), 5 July 1974.

36 See, for example, Khaddam's press conference, *Middle East News Agency (MENA)*, 4 June 1974; Deputy Premier, Muhamad Khaidar's interview to *Al-Musawar* (Cairo), 26 July 1974; Minister of Information, George Saddiqni's interview to *Svenska Dagbladet* (Stockholm), 9 August 1974.

37 *Damascus Domestic Service*, 16 June 1974; M. Ma'oz, *Syria Under Hafiz Al-Asad*, p. 25.

38 R.O. Freedman, *Soviet Policy towards the Middle East since 1970*, revised edition (New York: Praeger, 1978), p. 163; Asad's 5 July 1974 interview with *Al-Ahram*; Khaidar's 26 July interview with *Al-Musawar*.

39 *The Sunday Times*, 5 May 1974; *The Financial Times*, 30 August 1974.

40 G. Golan and I. Rabinovich, 'The Soviet Union and Syria: The Limits of Co-operation', in Y. Ro'i (ed.), *The Limits to Power* (London: Croom Helm, 1979), p. 221.

41 Asad's meeting with Brezhnev took place during his stopover in Moscow *en route* to North Korea. For description of the discussions, see: *Tass*, 27 September 1974; *Pravda*, 28 September 1974; *New Times*, No. 40 (1974), p. 5; *Damascus Domestic Service*, 28 September, 3 October 1974.

Notes

42 See, for example, Syrian Information Minister, Ahmad Iskandar Ahmad's interviews with the *Bulgarian News Agency* (*BTA*), 11 October 1974, and the Lebanese newspaper, *Al-Safir*, 12 October 1974.

43 *Tass*, 3 February 1975.

44 In late 1974, however, in response to Egypt's more forthcoming approach towards the idea of reconvening Geneva, the Soviets agreed to conclude a limited arms deal, primarily covering aviation-related equipment and including modern aircraft (e.g., MiG-23, SU-20) the Egyptians had not utilized previously. See E. Karsh, *Soviet Arms Transfers to the Middle East in the 1970s*, JCSS Paper No. 22 (Tel Aviv: The Jaffee Center for Strategic Studies, 1983), p. 10.

45 *Moscow Domestic Service in Russian*, 11 October 1974.

46 I. Belayev, 'Who Is Inflaming the Hotbed of Tension?', *Za Rubezhom*, 28 February – 6 March 1975, pp. 10–11.

47 L. Tolkunov, 'The Near East: Roots of Crisis and the Road to its Solution', *Kommunist*, No. 13 (September 1974), p. 105.

48 *Damascus Domestic Service*, 14 October 1974.

49 *DPA(Cairo), 14, 15 October 1974*. For further details on Kissinger's talks in Damascus, see: *Damascus Domestic Service*, 11, 14 October, 7 November 1974; *MENA* (Cairo), 7 November 1974; *New York Times*, 19 November 1974.

50 See, for example, *Al-Thawra*, 1, 20 February 1975; *Damascus Domestic Service*, 22 March 1975; *Al-Ba'th*, 26 March 1975; *Radio Peace and Progress in Arabic*, 11 February, 5, 10 March 1975; *Tass*, 26 February, 5, 13 March 1975; *Sovyetskaya Rossiya*, 7 March 1975; D. Antonov, 'Urgent Task', *New Times*, No. 7 (February 1975), p. 6.

51 *Jerusalem Post*, 15 December 1974; *SANA* (Damascus), 4 March 1975.

52 *Amman Domestic Service*, 15 March 1975.

53 Israel also suggested more limited territorial concessions in return for 'a general statement about the readiness to limit the use of force' and 'certain practical expressions ... of a movement towards peace'. This proposal was also rejected by Sadat.

54 See, for example, *Damascus Domestic Service*, 11 May, 1 June 1975; *Al-Thawra*, 22 June, 12 July 1975; *Moscow in Arabic*, 20, 27 June 1975; *Izvestiya*, 29 May 1975.

55 E. R. F. Sheehan, *The Arabs, Israelis, and Kissinger* (New York: Reader's Digest Press, 1976), p. 196; Ba'th Party Statement on the Disengagement Agreement, *Damascus Domestic Service*, 3 September 1975.

56 See, for example, Asad's interviews with *Time*, 1 December 1975, and *Newsweek*, 14 September 1975. See also *The Financial Times*, 13 October 1975.

57 See, for example, Asad's speech on the anniversary of the October War, *Damascus Domestic Service*, 6 October 1975; Sheehan, *The Arabs*, p. 196; *The Times*, 2 October 1975; *Tass*, 9 November 1975.

58 Asad's interview with *Al-Rai Al-Amm* (Kuwait), 18 October 1975; *New York Times*, 26 October 1975; *Sunday Telegraph*, 12 October 1975.

Chapter 3

1 The decisions of the 'First All-Syrian Congress', published in Damascus on 2 July 1919, defined 'Greater Syria' as the area bounded by the Taurus Mountains to the north, Aqaba and Rafah to the south, the Mediterranean to the West and the Euphrates and Khabur rivers to the east. These boundaries included today's Syria, Lebanon, Jordan and Israel. The roots of the concept of 'Greater Syria' can be traced back to the days of the Ummayad Caliphate, when the vast land north of Hijaz ('Bilad Al-Sha'm', the Northern Country) con- stituted a separate political entity.

2 Asad's 20 July 1976 speech on the Lebanese crisis; Asad's interviews with *Al-Hawadith* (Beirut), 26 June 1975; *Events* (London), 1 October 1976.

3 Asad's 20 July speech.

4 *Ibid.*

5 M. Tlas, *Al-Gazw Al-Israili Li Lubnan* (Damascus: Tishrin, 1983), p. 199.

6 *Al-Rai Al-Amm*, 7 January 1976.

7 *SANA*, 25 September 1975; *Al-Hawadith*, 12 December 1975; *Al-Safir* (Beirut), 21 May 1976. These forces were deployed near the northern town of Tripoli in an attempt to end the fighting there.

8 *Radio Moscow in Arabic*, 10, 11 October 1975.

9 *Pravda*, 12 October 1975; *Izvestiya*, 21, October 1975; *Radio Peace and Progress in Arabic*, 22 October 1975.

10 *Radio Peace and Progress in Arabic*, 25 September 1975.

11 See, for example, statements by Defence Minister Peres in *Ma'ariv*, 22, 26 March 1976 (Tel Aviv). Another factor that reinforced Israeli tolerance towards Syria's growing military intervention in Lebanon was the assumption that this intervention would reduce the Syrian ability and willingness to launch war or, alternatively, to obstruct a move towards a political settlement.

12 *Pravda*, 18 March 1976; *Tass*, 21 March 1976.

13 *Pravda*, 18, 29 May 1976.

14 *Radio Peace and Progress in Arabic*, 28 May 1976.

15 For such views see: Golan and Rabinovich, *The Soviet Union and Syria*, p. 226; R. Freedman, *Soviet Policy*, pp. 242–244; P. Ramet,

Notes

'The Soviet-Syrian Relationship', *Problems of Communism*, September-October 1986, p. 38.

16 A similar argument is presented in I. Kass's *The Lebanon Civil War 1975–1976: A Case of Crisis Mismanagement* (Jerusalem: The Hebrew University, 1979), pp. 18, 37–39. There is, nevertheless, no evidence whatsoever for her assumption regarding Soviet-Syrian complicity, let alone collusion, in the intervention in Lebanon.

17 A. Dawisha, *Syria and the Lebanese Crisis* (New York: St Martin's Press, 1980), p. 134.

18 *Al-Nahar Arab Report*, 7, No. 21 (24 May 1976).

19 *Damascus Domestic Service*, 2, 4 June 1976.

20 K. Dawisha, *Soviet Foreign Policy towards Egypt*, p. 78. See also *Guardian*, 3 May 1977; *Al Akhbar* (Jordan), 15 March 1977.

21 *Damascus Domestic Service*, 3 June 1976.

22 *Tass*, 5, 7 June 1976; *Pravda*, 6, 7, 8 June 1976; *Izvestiya*, 7 June 1976.

23 *International Herald Tribune*, 5 May 1976.

24 *Tass*, 9 June 1976.

25 A. Dawisha, *Syria and the Lebanese Crisis*, p. 149.

26 I. Kass, *The Lebanon Civil War*, p. 42.

27 *Radio Moscow in English*, 27 August 1976.

28 *Egyptian Gazette*, 13 June 1976.

29 See, for example, *Tass*, 6, 7, 8 July 1976 (Khaddam's visit); *Beirut Domestic Service*, 25 July 1976; *The Financial Times*, 9 August 1976 (Kuznetzov's visit).

30 *Le Monde*, 20 July 1976 (emphasis added).

31 *The Financial Times*, 9, 10 August 1976; *INA* (Baghdad), 15 July 1976.

32 *Damascus Domestic Service*, 10 June 1976.

33 *Ibid.*, 18, 20 June 1976.

34 *Ibid.*, 1 July 1976.

35 *Ibid.*, 12 August 1976.

36 *Ibid.*, 12 October 1976.

37 The Soviet peace initiative was made public on 1 October 1976. The extent of Soviet interest in mobilizing Syrian support for this plan was shown by the talks held by Vladimir Vinogradov in Damascus in September. For Vinogradov's visit see *The Financial Times*, 22 September 1976.

38 *New York Times*, 2 October 1976.

39 See, for example, *Pravda*, 7, 27 September 1976.

40 Interestingly enough, the statement summarizing Kadoumi's visit bore no reference to Syria's military intervention, nor did it contain a demand for Syrian withdrawal. See *Pravda*, 18 September 1976.

110

41 *Radio Moscow in Arabic*, 30 September 1976.
42 See, for example, *Tass*, 2, 10 October 1976; *Krasnaya Zvezda*, 3 October 1976; *Pravda*, 3, 7 October 1976.
43 See, for example, *Pravda*, 14, 17 October 1976; *Radio Peace and Progress in Arabic*, 18 October 1976.
44 Y. Tsaplin, 'Teaming Up', *New Times*, No. 48 (1976), p. 23.
45 E. Karsh, *Soviet Arms Transfers*, pp. 13–14.

Chapter 4
1 Asad's interview with Patrick Seale, *Observer*, 6 March 1977.
2 Asad's interview with *Time* magazine, as brought by *Damascus Domestic Service*, 17 January 1977.
3 *Izvestiya*, 1, 8 January 1977.
4 Asad's interview with Patrick Seale, *Observer*, 6 March 1977.
5 See, for example, *Damascus Domestic Service*, 15, 20, 23 January 1977; *Al Ba'th*, 15 March 1977.
6 *The Financial Times*, 20 April 1977.
7 See, for example, *Al-Thawra*, 16, 20, 24 April 1977; *Tishrin*, 20 April; *Al-Ba'th*, 24 April; *Izvestiya*, 22, 23 April 1977; *Tass*, 18, 19, 21, 22 April 1977; *Moscow Domestic Service in Russian*, 18, 19 April 1977.
8 *Tass*, 22 April 1977; *SANA* (Damascus), 28 June 1977; P. Cockburn, 'Political obstacles hinder plans for increased trade', *Middle East Economic Digest (MEED)*, 16 September 1977, p. 11.
9 *Tass*, 22 April 1977.
10 *Damascus Domestic Service*, 9 May 1977.
11 Y. Tyunkov, 'USSR-Syria: Strengthening co-operation', *New Times*, No. 18 (April 1977), p. 7.
12 *Damascus Domestic Service*, 4, 12 August 1977.
13 The Syrian Minister of Information, Ahmad Iskandar Ahmad's interview with *Al-Rai Al-Amm* (Kuwait), 14 February 1978. See also Abd Al-Khalim Khaddam's declarations, as brought by *Damascus Domestic Service*, 17 December 1977, 13, 24, 27 January 1978.
14 See, for example, *Tass*, 17–20 November 1977; *Moscow in Arabic*, 17, 28 November 1977; *Pravda*, 17, 19 November 1977.
15 See, for example, *Krasnaya Zvezda*, 2 December 1977; *Tass*, 5 December 1977, 10 February 1978; *Pravda*, 4, 5 February 1978; *Moscow in Arabic*, 2 December 1977, 6, 7 February 1978. The Front consisted of Syria, Libya, Algeria, South Yemen and the PLO.
16 The request was made during Grechko's visit to Damascus. See *International Herald Tribune*, 13 May 1972.

17 See *DPA* (Cairo), 6 August 1972; Asad's interview with *Al-Anwar*, 10 August 1972, and with *Al-Rai Al-Amm* (Kuwait), 18 October 1975.

18 Asad's interview with *Al-Rai Al-Amm*, 18 October 1975.

19 *Damascus Domestic Service*, 8 March 1980.

20 *The Financial Times*, 8 September 1978.

21 *Al-Mustaqbal* (Paris), 16 December 1978.

22 This intention found a clear echo in Brezhnev's speech honouring Asad: 'We are ... prepared to more widely extend the framework of our all-round cooperation and, above all, in the political sphere.' See *Moscow Domestic Service in Russian*, 5 October 1978.

23 If anything, the Soviet refusal reflected Moscow's apprehensions over the implications of the sudden Syrian-Iraqi reconciliation of late 1978. Enabling Syria to face Israel on its own was one thing, but the Soviets were reluctant to provide the same sophisticated weapons systems to a more powerful Syrian-Iraqi union, which might launch a military campaign or provoke Israel to risk a pre-emptive strike. Thus Shihabi was not the only one to be turned down by the Soviets; the Iraqi Minister of Defence, Adnan Khair- Allah, returned empty-handed from Moscow in November 1978.

24 For the text of the communiqué, see *Tass*, 26 March 1979.

25 See, for example, *Trud*, 30 March 1979; *Moscow in Arabic*, 17 April, 22 May 1979; *Pravda*, 28 March, 12 April 1979; *Tass*, 19 April 1979.

26 *The Financial Times*, 15 October 1979.

27 *Al-Mustaqbal* (Paris), 3 November 1979.

28 The data presented in this study regarding arms procurement constitute an aggregate, based upon a rather wide variety of sources. It has, therefore, generally avoided indicating specific references. Apart from numerous military journals, primary sources are: the yearbooks of the London-based International Institute for Strategic Studies – *Strategic Survey, The Military Balance*; the Tel Aviv-based Jaffee Center for Strategic Studies' yearbook – *Middle East Military Balance*; the annual publication of the Stockholm-based Institute for Peace Research (SIPRI) – *World Armament and Disarmament*; the US Arms Control and Disarmament Agency publication – *World Military Expenditures and Arms Transfers*.

29 See, for example, *Pravda*, 17 February, 17 March, 17 April, 17 June, 11, 13 July 1980; *Izvestiya*, 3, 6 June 1980; *Krasnaya Zvezda*, 11 June 1980; *Tass*, 17, 21 March, 23 September 1980; *Moscow in Arabic*, 7 March 1980.

30 At the UN discussion, South Yemen voted against the resolution (i.e., in favour of the USSR), Syria and Algeria abstained and Libya was absent from the deliberations.

31 *Associated Press*, 29 January 1980.

32 *Tass*, 29 January 1980.
33 *Damascus Domestic Service*, 18 February 1980.
34 *Ibid.*, 15 March 1980.
35 *Ibid.*, 23 April 1980.
36 See, for example, Khaddam's interview with *Kuwait News Agency* (*Kuna*), as brought by *Tishrin*, 17 May 1980; Khaddam's interview with *Al-Nahar Al-Arabi Wa Al-Duwali* (Paris), 28 July-3 August 1980; Ahmad's interview with *Qatar News Agency* (*QNA*) (Doha), 25 August 1980 and with *Al-Anwar*, 24 September 1980; *Tishrin*, 25, 27 June, 13 July, 1 August 1980.
37 Within this framework, the Syrian Minister of Defence, Tlas, was reported to have visited Moscow in late May, while the Commander of the Soviet Navy, Admiral Sergei Gorshkov, visited Damascus in early July.
38 *SANA*, 17 May 1980 (Khaddam's interview); *Damascus Domestic Service*, 25 August 1980 (Ba'th Congress).

Chapter 5

1 Ahamd's interview with *Monday Morning* (Beirut), as brought by *Damascus Domestic Service*, 9 November 1980.
2 See, for example, *Pravda*, 3 December 1980; *Moscow Domestic Service in Russian*, 12 October 1980.
3 *Tass*, 8 October 1980 (emphasis added).
4 See, for example, *Tass*, 25 November 1980; *Radio Moscow in Arabic*, 16 December 1980.
5 See, for example, *Tass*, 6 December 1980.
6 See: *Tass*, 2 December 1980; *Pravda*, 3 December 1980; *Damascus Domestic Service*, 2 December 1980.
7 See interview of the Israeli Chief of Staff, Refael Eitan, on *Israeli television*, 14 May 1981.
8 *Tass*, 5 May 1981; *Pravda, Moscow Domestic Service in Russian*, 17 May 1981.
9 Kornienko's welcome address, as brought by *Damascus Domestic Service*, 6 May 1981. See also *Radio Peace and Progress in Arabic*, 11, 20 May 1981.
10 *Voice of Lebanon*, 19 May 1981. Egyptian Vice-President, Husni Mubarak's interview with *Ma'ariv* (Tel Aviv), 25 May 1981. Asad's visit to the USSR's was later denied by Abd Al-Khalim Khaddam – *SANA* (Damascus), 1 June 1981.
11 *IDF Radio* (Tel Aviv), 13 May 1981; *Washington Post*, 16 May 1981; *Daily Telegraph*, 3, 4 July 1981.

12 *Tass*, 14 May 1981; *The Financial Times*, 3 June 1981.
13 *Daily Telegraph*, 4, 7 July 1981; *The Financial Times*, 6, 7 July 1981.
14 *Radio Monte Carlo in Arabic*, 8 May 1981.
15 Soviet Ambassador to Lebanon, Alexander Soldatov, as cited by *Beirut Domestic Service*, 14 May 1981; see also *Moscow television*, 16 May 1981.
16 *Pravda*, 23 May 1981.
17 See, for example, *Moscow Domestic Service in Russian*, 14, 17 May 1981.
18 *Literaturnaya Gazeta*, 6 May 1981.
19 *Damascus Domestic Service*, 18 May 1981.
20 Soldatov, as cited by *Beirut Domestic Service*, 16 May 1981.
21 *Tass*, 28 May 1981.
22 *Ibid.*, 26 May 1981.
23 See, for example, Asad's interview with *Budapest television*, 28 June 1981, with *Al-Rai Al-Amm* (Kuwait), 13 December 1981.
24 Khaddam's interview with *Al-Nahar Al-Arabi Wa Al Duwali*, as brought by *SANA*, 6 June 1981.
25 Asad's interview with *ABC*, *NBC* and *CBS* television networks, as well as with *Stern* magazine, as brought by *Damascus Domestic Service*, 21 May and 8 June 1981 respectively.
26 *Al-Majallah* (London), 11–17 July 1981, pp. 42–3.
27 Asad's interview with *Al-Rai Al-Amm* (Kuwait), 13 December 1981.
28 *Tishrin*, 1 October 1981.
29 *Al-Watan* (Kuwait), 21 November 1981. Indirect evidence of the Soviet refusal to increase military support for Syria can also be found in Asad's interview with *Al-Rai Al-Amm* on 13 December.
30 *Radio Peace and Progress in Hebrew*, 25 September 1981; *Radio Moscow in English*, 6 October 1981.
31 See, for example, *Pravda*, 16 December 1981, 6, 10 January 1982; *Tass*, 18, 19 December 1981.
32 See, for example, Syrian Deputy Foreign Minister, Nasir Qaddur's interview with *Radio Monte Carlo in Arabic*, 18 December 1981.
33 The fact that Syria requested a strategic pact during Khaddam's visit is substantiated by Khaddam's interview with *Al Sharq al-Awsat* (Kuwait), 6 January 1982. See also Ahmad's interviews with *Monday Morning* and *Guardian*, 15 January 1982.
34 Syrian government statement, *Damascus Domestic Service*, 16 December 1982.
35 Ahmad's press interview as reported by *Radio Monte Carlo in Arabic*, 17 December 1981.
36 I. Rabinovich, 'The Changing Prism: Syrian Policy in Lebanon as a Mirror, an Issue and an Instrument', in M. Ma'oz and A. Yaniv

(eds.), *Syria Under Hafiz Asad* (New York: St. Martin's Press, 1986), pp. 185–6.
37 Z. Schiff and E. Ya'ari, *Israel's Lebanon War* (London: Allen & Unwin, 1984), pp. 42–4.
38 *Tass*, 22 April 1982.
39 *Soviet television*, 8 June 1982.
40 G. Golan, 'The Soviet Union and the Israeli Action in Lebanon', *International Affairs*, Vol. 59, No. 1 (Winter 1982/83), p. 7.
41 R.O. Freedman, 'The Soviet Union and the Middle East: Failure to Match the United States as a Superpower', in C. Legum *et al.* (eds.), *Middle East Contemporary Survey* (*MECS*) (New York: Holmes & Meier, 1984), Vol. 6, 1981–2, p. 43.
42 *Ha'aretz* (Tel Aviv), 16 June 1982; *Ma'ariv* (Tel Aviv), 28 June *Al-Hamishmar* (Tel Aviv), 9 June 1982.
43 *Damascus Domestic Service*, 13 June 1982; *QNA* (Doha), 15 June 1982.
44 *Israeli television*, 24 June 1982.
45 *Ma'ariv*, 8 April 1983.
46 See, for example, *Radio Peace and Progress*, 8 June 1982.
47 *International Herald Tribune*, 11 June 1982; *New York Times*, 30 June 1982.
48 *New York Times*, 11 June 1982.
49 *Tass*, 7 June 1982.
50 *Ibid.*, 14 June 1982 (emphasis added).
51 There has always been the possibility of influencing the course of a specific war through direct military intervention, as the USSR did in the Egyptian-Israeli War of Attrition in 1970. Nonetheless, this extraordinary intervention was undertaken half-heartedly and in the face of an Egyptian ultimatum, thereby reflecting the extreme limits, rather than the norm, of Soviet military intervention. For a detailed discussion of the nature and characteristics of Soviet military engagement in Middle Eastern wars, as well as their limitations, see E. Karsh, *The Cautious Bear: Soviet Military Engagement in Middle East Wars in the Post-1967 Era* (Boulder and Jerusalem: Westview Press and The Jerusalem Post Press, 1985) and 'The Myth of Direct Soviet Intervention in an Arab-Israeli War', *RUSI Journal*, Vol. 129, No. 3 (September 1984), pp. 28–32.
52 Schiff and Ya'ari, *Israel's Lebanon War*, p. 57.
53 *Damascus Domestic Service*, 19 June 1982.
54 *Damascus television*, 21 June 1982. For further praise of the Soviet friendship and support see, for example, Ahmad Iskandar Ahamd's news conference (Damascus television), *Damascus Domestic Service*, 20, 27 June 1982; *Al-Thawra*, 4 August 1982.

55 For Syria's pronounced interest in a defence pact see, for example, Iskandar's abovementioned news conference, as well as his interview with *Pravda*, 20 June 1982.

56 On 1 September 1982, President Reagan made an important speech calling for a new initiative on the settlement of the Arab-Israeli conflict. Modelled, by and large, on US Middle Eastern policy, Reagan's peace plan envisaged an Israeli withdrawal to the pre-1967 border, with some revisions, in exchange for a peace settlement. Rejecting the idea of an independent Palestinian state, Reagan suggested 'self-government by the Palestinians of the West Bank and Gaza in association with Jordan'.

57 C. Roberts, 'Soviet Arms-Transfer Policy and the Decision to Upgrade Syrian Air Defences', *Survival*, July-August 1982, p. 155.

58 *Ibid.*, p. 156.

59 *Pravda*, 21 July 1982 (Brezhnev's initiative); *Tass*, 28 August 1982 (Syrian support for the initiative).

Chapter 6

1 *MECS*, 1982–3, p. 817.

2 For the view that the Soviet commitment to Syria's security, in accordance with the 1980 treaty, did not apply to Lebanon, see Alexander Soldatov's comments as brought by *Beirut Domestic Service*, 2 March 1983.

3 *Moscow in Arabic*, 14 February 1983; *Radio Peace and Progress in Arabic*, 2 March 1983.

4 For the impact of the Soviet assurances on Syrian morale, see, for example, *Tishrin*, 31 January, 28 February, 28 March 1983.

5 *Damascus Domestic Service*, 17 November 1982.

6 Schiff and Ya'ari, *Israel's Lebanon War*, p. 295.

7 *Tass*, 23 November 1982.

8 For further Soviet appeals to the PLO implying indirect criticism, see, for example, the telegram sent to Arafat by the Soviet leadership on 28 November 1982, on the occasion of the international solidarity day with the Palestinian people: *Moscow Domestic Service in Russian*, 28 November 1982.

9 *International Herald Tribune*, 24–25 September 1983; *Guardian*, 14 May, 9 June 1983; *The Times*, 9, 10 June 1983.

10 Moreover, on 4 December 1983 the United States suffered a public humiliation, when two of its aircraft were shot down by the Syrians, with one pilot killed and the other captured. The captured airman was released in January 1984 following a highly publicized visit of the Democratic presidential candidate, Jesse Jackson, to Damascus.

11 See, for example, *Radio Moscow in English*, 14 May 1983; *Tass*, 9 June 1983.

12 *Moscow television*, 11 May 1983; *Radio Moscow in English*, 14 May 1983.

13 *Pravda*, 12 May 1983.

14 *Radio Moscow in English*, 11 May 1983; D. Zgersky, 'Syria A Target', *New Times*, No. 48 (November 1983), p. 15.

15 *Foreign Report*, 30 June 1983; *Washington Post*, 7, 9 October 1983.

16 For Soviet pressure on the PLO see, for example, *Tass*, 13 July 1983; *The Times*, 27 June 1983; *Washington Post*, 17 July 1983; *MECS*, 1982–3, p. 314.

17 For Soviet pressure on Syria see, for example, the joint communiqué issued at the close of Khaddam's visit to Moscow: *Tass*, 11 November 1983. See also *Christian Science Monitor*, 17 November 1983.

18 *Pravda*, 19 November 1983.

19 The only crisis when the Soviet-Syrian treaty was given salience by Moscow was the 'Golan Crisis' following the Israeli annexation of the Golan Heights in December 1981. Yet as the escalatory potential of this crisis was very small, the reference to the treaty did not imply any Soviet military commitment to Syria's security; rather, it served as a signal to Syria of the benefits of the treaty, so as to forestall the conclusion of a defence pact.

20 A. Stepanov, 'USSR-Syria: Consistent Support', *New Times*, No. 42 (October 1983), p. 13.

21 *Pravda*, 13 November 1983.

22 See, for example, *Soviet television*, 25 July 1983 (Prime Minister Kasm's interview); *SANA*, 12 October 1983 (Asad's views); *Pravda*, 13 November 1983.

23 See, for example, R.O. Freedmam, 'Moscow, Damascus and the Lebanese Crisis of 1982–1984', *Middle East Review*, Vol. 17, No. 1 (Fall 1984), p. 35.

24 *Al-Yamama* (Saudi Arabia), 30 March 1983.

25 *MEED*, 15 April 1983.

26 The TU-154 purchase cost Syria $51.6 million: *Al-Thawra*, 5 March 1983; *Guardian*, 14 May 1983.

27 For the Soviet peace plan see *Pravda*, 30 July 1984.

28 See, for example, *Radio Moscow in Arabic*, 28 April 1984.

29 In March 1984, for the first time since becoming president in March 1971, Hafiz Asad nominated three vice-presidents: Abd Al-Khalim Khaddam, the former foreign minister; Rif'at Asad, the president's brother, and Zuhair Mashariqa, a Ba'th official of a lower standing. Directly related to Asad's health problems, this move confirmed the existence of a power struggle within the Syrian leadership. For the

decree announcing the changes see *Damascus Domestic Service*, 11 March 1984.

30 *Tass*, 29 May 1984; *SANA*, 29 May 1984. For further Soviet and Syrian accounts of the visit see, for example, *Moscow in Arabic*, 25 May, 2 June 1984; *Tass*, 28 May 1984; *Damascus Domestic Service*, 29 May 1984. For Western accounts see: *Guardian*, 30 May, 4 June 1984; *The Times*, 31 May, 1 June 1984.

31 While Andropov was in power, Asad did not pay an official visit to the USSR, though he was reported to have gone on two secret visits. *International Herald Tribune*, 17 February 1984.

32 *Al-Watan Al-Arabi* (Beirut), 9 November 1984.

33 *Ibid.; Al-Watan* (Kuwait), 13 October 1984. Moscow's pressures on Syria with regard to the Iran-Iraq War reflected growing apprehensions about an Iraqi collapse, on the one hand, and a modest improvement in Soviet-Iranian relations which reduced Damascus's importance as a back-channel to Tehran, on the other.

34 See the joint communiqué issued at the close of the visit, *Pravda*, 19 October 1984.

35 *Radio Moscow in English*, 17 October 1984. While the Soviet-Syrian joint communiqué contained no reference to Soviet relations with other Arab countries, *Pravda*'s report of the 18 October Politburo meeting reiterated this linkage. Also, the Soviets were reported to have evaded Asad's request for a moratorium on Syria's military debt. *Foreign Report* (London), 22 November 1984, p. 8.

36 Indeed in late 1984 the Soviets signed an arms deal with Jordan. L.C. Napper, 'The Arab Autumn of 1984: A Case Study of Soviet Middle East Diplomacy', *Middle East Journal*, Vol. 39, No. 4 (Autumn 1985), p. 743.

37 For the evacuation of the Soviet forces from Syria see, for example, *New York Times*, 26 January 1986; *Jane's Defence Weekly*, 11, 25 May 1985.

38 *Radio Monte Carlo*, 6 October 1984; *Al Hawadith* (London), 12 October 1984, pp. 27–9.

39 See, for example, Mustafa Tlas's interview with *Libération* (Paris), 30 November 1984, p. 25; *Daily Telegraph*, 29 November 1984.

40 Napper, *The Arab Autumn*, pp. 742–3.

41 It should be noted that Bovin also emphasized Syria's 'repeated indication' of the temporary basis of its presence in Lebanon. Yet the overall context of the article left little doubt that this reference did not imply the need for a Syrian withdrawal from Lebanon, but rather was intended to praise Damascus for its lack of territorial ambitions towards that country.

42 *Radio Peace and Progress in Arabic*, 21 February 1985; see also

Pravda, 1 January, 28 February 1985; *Tass*, 27 January 1985; O.
Fomin, 'Palestinian Rights: Two Lines', *New Times*, No. 12 (March
1985), pp. 22–3; O. Fomin, 'Trying to Revive the Camp David Deal',
New Times, No. 18 (April 1985), pp. 14–15.
43 E. Karsh, 'Soviet-Israeli Relations: A New Phase?', *The World Today*,
Vol. 41, No. 12 (December 1985), pp. 214–7.
44 These included, *inter alia*, meetings between the Soviet and Israeli
foreign ministers during discussions at the United Nations General
Assembly in September 1986 and September 1987.
45 See, for example, *Pravda*, 2 February 1988; Gennady Gerasimov's
interview with Israeli radio, *Jerusalem Domestic Service in Hebrew*, 20
January 1988.
46 G. Golan, 'The Soviet Union and the PLO since the War in
Lebanon', *Middle East Journal*, Vol. 40, No. 2 (Spring 1986), p. 305.
47 For further discussion of Syria's economic problems see E.
Kanovsky's paper, *What's Behind Syria's Current Economic Problems?*
(Tel Aviv: The Dayan Centre, 1985).
48 A glimpse into the turbulence within the regime was afforded in
January 1987 by the jailing of General Muhammad Al-Khouly, head
of the Syrian Air Force Intelligence and the most influential person in
Damascus after Asad; he was believed to be behind the failed attempt
to blow up an Israeli El-Al airplane in London in April 1986. See
Guardian, 22 January 1987.
49 In December 1985, following the downing of two of its aircraft by the
Israeli air force on 19 November in a dogfight over the Beq'a, Syria
positioned some SA-2 surface-to-air missile batteries along its border
with Lebanon and, moreover, deployed a few SA-6 and SA-8 mobile
surface-to-air missile batteries on Lebanese territory. An open
defiance of Israel's unwritten 'red lines', which excluded the introduction of Syrian surface-to-air missiles into Lebanon, this move created
an immediate resurgence of tension between Israel and Syria.
Although in early January 1986 Syria withdrew the mobile missiles
from Lebanon, Israel remained uneasy about the presence of the SA-2
batteries on the Syrian-Lebanese border; they severely constrained the
IAF flights over Lebanon. Yet, in order to avoid escalation, Israeli
reconnaissance flights over Lebanon were moved westward.
50 *New York Times*, 24, 25 April 1986.
51 For Asad's June 1985 visit see, for example, *Tass*, 19, 23 June 1985;
Pravda, 20 June 1985; *Le Monde*, 21 June 1985. 42; *Moscow Domestic
Service in Russian*, 27, 28 December 1985.
52 *Moscow Domestic Service in Russian*, 27, 28 December 1985.
53 See, for example, *Pravda*, 29 December 1985.
54 *Radio Moscow in Arabic*, 16 May 1986.

55 This warning was voiced a day before Khaddam's arrival, during Gorbachev's meeting with a group of British parliamentarians. *The Financial Times*, 23 November 1986.

56 See, for example, *Moscow television*, 28 May 1986; *Tass*, 28 May 1986; *Damascus Domestic Service*, 28 May 1986; *The Financial Times*, 3 June 1986; *Guardian*, 29 May 1986.

57 *Izvestiya*, 30 May 1986.

58 *Tass*, 28 May, 1 June 1986.

59 *Al Mustaqbal* (Paris), 14 June 1986, p. 10.

60 In February 1986 Iran made its first gain of Iraqi territory by occupying the peninsula of Fao on the south-eastern tip of Iraq; in early July Iran retook the town of Mehran on the central front, captured by Iraq a couple of months earlier, and in September Iranian forces made moderate gains on the northern front.

61 See, for example, *Izvestiya*, 28 October 1985; Brutents's comments to *Al Ba'th*, 3 November 1985.

62 See, for example, Asad's interview with *Libération*, 14 February 1986, with *Moscow television*, 27 April 1986; Vice-President Mashariqa's interview with *Al Ba'th*, 16 November 1987; see also *Damascus Domestic Service*, 3 January, 16, 21 March, 2 April, 18 October 1987.

63 For Soviet accounts of Asad's talks with Gorbachev see: *Moscow Domestic Service in Russian*, 24 April 1987; joint Soviet-Syrian statement on Asad's visit, *Tass*, 26 April 1987; Y. Potomov, 'USSR-Syria: Realistic Approach', *New Times*, No. 18 (May 1987), p. 8. See also *New York Times*, 30 April 1987.

64 See, for example, *Guardian*, 24 July 1987; *Ma'ariv* (Tel Aviv), 22, 23 July 1987.

65 *Tass*, 26 April 1987.

66 V. Zhitomirsky, 'A Splendid View of Syria', *New Times*, No. 31 (August 1987), p. 5.

67 *Moscow Domestic Serivce in Russian*, 24 April 1987.

68 Potomov, *USSR-Syria*, p. 8.

69 *Moscow Domestic Serivce in Russian*, 24 April 1987.

70 *Tass*, 26 April 1987; *Moscow Domestic Service in Russian*, 24 April 1987.

71 *Ibid.*

72 Asad's interview with the *Washington Post*, as brought by *Damascus Domestic Service*, 21 September 1987.

Chapter 7

1 In the first half of the 1980s, sub-Saharan Africa received Soviet military support totalling $6,075 billion, East Asia $4,950 billion and Latin America $4,150 billion.

2 M. Handel, *Weak States in the International System* (London: Frank Cass, 1971), pp. 132–5. To be sure, there are those who, by adopting the so-called 'client-centric' approach, emphasize the bargaining power of the client *vis-à-vis* the patron and go so far as to include cases of unilateral dependence of the patron on the client within the patron-client paradigm. Such views, nevertheless, fail to comprehend the essence of the concept of patron (or alternatively, client) which, originating in the Latin *pater*, implies preponderance, authority and seniority. Hence, any relationship clearly favouring the weaker partner *ipso facto* falls within the boundaries of the *power of the weak*, or *the tail wags the dog* paradigm. For a recent study of Soviet relations with a small allied state, see P. Shearman, *The Soviet Union and Cuba* (London: RIIA/RKP, 1987).

3 S. Hoffmann, *Gulliver's Troubles, Or the Setting of American Foreign Policy* (New York: McGraw Hill, 1968), pp. 39, 53.

4 Ramet, *The Soviet-Syrian Relationship*, p. 46.

5 D. Pipes, 'Syria: The Cuba of the Middle East?', *Commentary*, July 1986, pp. 16–17.

6 R.O. Freedman, 'Moscow, Damascus and the Lebanon Crisis', in M. Ma'oz and A. Yaniv (eds.), *Syria Under Asad*, p. 243.

7 A. Dawisha, *The Arab Radicals* (New York: Council on Foreign Relations, 1986), p. 34.

8 *Observer*, 7 March 1982.

9 See, for example, Asad's interview with *Libération* (Paris), 14 February 1986.

10 *Al Ba'th*, 23 June 1985.

11 For Syria's view of the Arab-Israeli conflict see, for example, Asad's interview with *Al-Nahar* (Beirut), 17 March 1971; speech on Lebanon, *Damascus Domestic Service*, 20 July 1976; interview for the Kuwaiti press, as brought by *Damascus Domestic Service*, 13 December 1981; speech at a revolution anniversary rally, *Damascus Domestic Service*, 7 March 1982; interview with *Libération* (Paris), 14 February 1986. See also Vice-President Khaddam's interview with *Monday Morning* (Beirut), 14–20 May 1979; comments on the conflict, as cited by *SANA*, 4 February 1978. See also Vice-President Zuhair Mashariqa's interview with *Al- Ba'th*, 24 January 1987, 8 March 1987. See also statement of the 13th National Congress of the Ba'th Party, *Damascus Domestic Service*, 25 August 1980.

12 M. Gorbachev, *Perestroika: New Thinking for our Country and the World* (New York: Pergamon, 1987), p. 174.

APPENDICES

Appendix 1 The Treaty of Friendship and Cooperation between the Union of Soviet Socialist Republics and the Syrian Arab Republic

The Union of Soviet Socialist Republics and the Syrian Arab Republic, inspired by the wish to develop and strengthen relations of friendship and all-round cooperation that have formed between them, in the interests of the people of both states, of the cause of security over the world, of consolidation of international detente, and development of peaceful cooperation among states,

Determined to give a firm rebuff to the policy of aggression conducted by imperialism and its accomplices, to continue the struggle against colonialism, neocolonialism and racism in all their forms and manifestations, including Zionism, to come out for national independence and social progress,

Attaching great significance to the continuation of cooperation of both countries in establishing a just and durable peace in the Middle East,

Confirming allegiance to the goals and principles of the charter of the United Nations organization, including the principles of respect for sovereignty, national independence, territorial integrity and noninterference in internal affairs,

Decided to conclude the present treaty and agreed on the following:

Article 1

The high contracting parties proclaim their resolve to develop steadily and strengthen friendship and cooperation between both states and people in the political, economic, military, scientific, technological, cultural and other spheres on the basis of the principles of equality, mutual advantage,

122

respect for sovereignty, national independence and territorial integrity, and noninterference in each other's internal affairs.

Article 2
The high contracting parties shall promote in every way the strengthening of universal peace and security of peoples, the relaxation of international tensions and their implementation in concrete forms of cooperation among states, the settlement of disputable questions by peaceful means, removing any manifestations of the policy of hegemonism and aggression from the practice of international relations.

The sides shall be cooperating intensively with each other in solving the tasks of ending the arms race, of achieving general and complete disarmament, including nuclear disarmament under effective international control.

Article 3
The high contracting parties, guided by their belief in the equality of all peoples and states, regardless of race and religious beliefs, condemn colonialism, racism and Zionism as one of the forms and manifestations of racism, and reaffirm their resolve to wage tireless struggle against them. The sides will be cooperating with other states in supporting just aspirations of peoples in their struggle against imperialism for ultimate and complete elimination of colonialism and racial domination, for freedom and social progress.

Article 4
The Union of Soviet Socialist Republics shall respect the policy of nonalignment pursued by the Syrian Arab Republic, which constitutes a major factor contributing to the preservation and consolidation of the international peace and security and to a lessening of international tensions.

The Syrian Arab Republic shall respect the peaceful foreign policy pursued by the Union of Soviet Socialist Republics, aimed at consolidating friendship and cooperation with all the countries and peoples.

Article 5
The high contracting parties shall develop and broaden the practice of mutual exchange of opinions and regular consultations on questions of bilateral relations and international problems of interest to both sides, and above all on the problems of the Middle East. Consultations and exchanges of opinion shall be held at different levels, above all through meetings of the leading states figures of both sides.

Article 6
In cases of the emergence of situations jeopardizing peace or security of one of the parties or posing a threat to peace or violating peace and security

in the whole world, the high contracting parties shall enter without delay into contact with each other with a view to coordinating their positions and to cooperation in order to remove the threat that has arisen and to restore the peace.

Article 7

The high contracting parties shall carry out close and comprehensive cooperation in assuring conditions for the preservation and development of the social and economic accomplishments of their peoples, for respecting the sovereignty of each of the two parties over their natural resources.

Article 8

The high contracting parties shall contribute to a steady consolidation and broadening of the mutually advantageous economic as well as scientific-technological cooperation and exchange of experience between them in the field of industry, agriculture, irrigation and water resources, utilization of oil and other natural resources, in the field of communications, transport and other economic sectors as well as in the training of national cadres. The sides undertake to broaden trade and maritime navigation between them on the basis of the principles of equality, mutual benefit and the most favoured nation treatment.

Article 9

The high contracting parties shall continue to develop their cooperation and exchange of experience in the fields of science, art, literature, education, health, information, cinematography, tourism, sports and other fields.

The sides undertake to contribute to the expansion of contacts and cooperation between the organs of state power and mass-affiliation organizations, including the trade union and other public organizations, enterprises and cultural and scientific establishments with a view to an increasingly more profound familiarization of the people of both countries with the life, work, experience and achievements of each other.

Article 10

The high contracting parties shall continue to develop cooperation in the military field on the basis of appropriate agreements concluded between them in the interests of strengthening of their defense capacity.

Article 11

Each of the high contracting parties states that it shall not enter into alliances or participate in any groupings of states as well as in activities directed against the other high contracting party.

Article 12

Each of the high contracting parties states that its obligations under the current international agreements do not contradict the provisions of this treaty, and undertakes not to conclude any international agreements which are incompatible with it.

Article 13

Any differences that may arise between the high contracting parties in the interpretation or application of any provision of this treaty shall be resolved on a bilateral basis, in the spirit of friendship, mutual understanding and respect.

Article 14

This treaty shall be effective for twenty years as of the day it enters into force.

If neither of the high contracting parties states six months prior to the expiry of the above mentioned period its desire to terminate the treaty, it shall remain effective for the next five years until one of the high contracting parties notifies in writing six months prior to the expiry of the current five-year period its intention to terminate it.

Article 15

This treaty is subject to ratification and shall enter into force on the day of the exchange of ratification instruments, which shall be done in Damascus.

Done in Moscow on October 8, 1980, in duplicate, each in Russian and Arabic languages, with both texts being equally authentic.

Appendix 2 Expansion of the Syrian armed forces, 1973–86

Military capability	October 1973	War losses	May 1975	October 1979	Mid-1982	War losses	1984	1986
Weapons Systems:								
Tanks	1,500	c. 1,000	2,200	2,600	4,000	c. 400	4,100	4,200
Armoured vehicles	1,000	unknown	1,200	1,600	3,500	few hundreds	3,500	3,600
Artillery pieces	900	c. 400	800	900	2,600	unknown	3,500	3,800
Surface-to-air missile batteries	30	15	40	50	100	c. 20	150	150
Combat aircraft	310	c. 200	350	400	600	90	650	650
Missile boats	8	5	9	14	18	—	22	24
Manpower and formations:								
Total manpower (in thousands)	132	—	150	247	310	—	400	500
Armoured divisions	2	—	2	2	4	—	5	5
Mechanized divisions	3	—	3	3	2	—	3	3
Independent brigades	5	—	4	9	10	—	17	10
Special operations division	—	—	—	—	—	—	—	1

Source: The Military Balance; various issues (London: The International Institute for Strategic Studies).

Appendix 3 Soviet trade with Syria (million US$)

Year	Soviet exports	Soviet imports	Soviet trade balance
1955	0.3	0.0	0.3
1956	1.6	1.6	0.0
1957	4.3	5.4	−1.1
1958	15.2	23.3	−8.1
1959	15.1	6.1	9.0
1960	11.0	7.8	3.2
1961	17.0	4.3	12.7
1962	5.2	6.9	−1.7
1963	13.1	14.2	−1.1
1964	12.2	17.8	−5.6
1965	12.7	18.6	−5.9
1966	22.7	20.3	2.3
1967	34.2	18.2	16.0
1968	42.1	20.9	21.2
1969	47.8	37.3	10.4
1970	46.4	19.2	27.2
1971	57.7	29.3	28.3
1972	71.1	65.2	5.9
1973	97.6	63.2	34.4
1974	92.5	135.0	−42.5
1975	137.5	95.6	41.9
1976	183.7	128.5	55.2
1977	136.8	144.1	−7.3
1978	192.7	108.4	84.3
1979	203.5	100.5	103.1
1980	258.2	236.4	21.9
1981	387.3	349.8	37.6
1982	290.4	414.3	−124.0
1983	275.9	403.6	−127.7
1984	305.5	269.0	36.5
1985	383.6	226.7	156.9

Source: Vneshnyaya Torgovlya USSR.

Forthcoming Related Titles

The Soviet Union and India
Peter J.S. Duncan

India is the only non-communist country in the Third World with which the Soviet Union has managed to maintain friendly relations over a prolonged period. To what extent is the closeness of India to the USSR on many policy issues the result of coincidence of interests rather than Soviet influence? The author assesses the balance of costs and benefits to the USSR of its considerable economic and military involvements with India; considers the effects of changing domestic, regional and global considerations, both on this balance and on the relationship in general; and concludes by looking at the implications of possible shifts in Soviet policy in the region for Western links with India.

Soviet Foreign Policy Priorities under Gorbachev
Alex Pravda

Gorbachev has clearly brought a more energetic and flexible style to the conduct of Soviet foreign policy, but has he altered its substance? This paper examines new elements in Soviet thinking about security and foreign policy priorities and the relative utility of military and political instruments in advancing them. It also assesses the effects of tightening domestic constraints and an increasingly difficult international environment. In order to gauge the extent of actual as distinct from declaratory shifts in priorities, the paper reviews recent policy towards the United States, Western Europe, the socialist bloc and major Asian states. Finally, it examines the policy implications of such shifts for the West in general and Western Europe in particular.

Soviet Policy Perspectives on Western Europe
Neil Malcolm

Under Gorbachev, Soviet diplomacy has sought to build closer relationships with regional power centres such as Western Europe. Has this meant a serious modification of the postwar focus of policy on relations with the United States? Are plans being forwarded to split the Atlantic alliance? This paper reviews Soviet specialist writing and leadership statements, and looks in particular at how Soviet authors understand the interplay of cooperation and conflict inside the European Community, and in the Western world as a whole. It concludes that the new thinking in Soviet policy is founded on a sober appreciation of the underlying cohesiveness and adaptability of the West, and on a determination to work with, rather than against, tendencies to integration.

ROUTLEDGE